COPING WITH
PANIC

A Drug-Free Approach to Dealing with Anxiety Attacks

COPING WITH
PANIC

A Drug-Free Approach to Dealing with Anxiety Attacks

George A. Clum
Virginia Polytechnic Institute and State University

Brooks/Cole Publishing Company
Pacific Grove, California

Brooks/Cole Publishing Company
A Division of Wadsworth, Inc.

Library of Congress Cataloging-in-Publication Data
Clum, George A., [date]
  Coping with panic.

  Bibliography: p.
  Includes index.
1. Panic attacks—Popular works.   I. Title.
RC535.C58 1990   616.85'223   89-9960
ISBN 0-534-11295-1

Sponsoring Editor: *Claire Verduin*
Editorial Assistant: *Gay C. Bond*
Production Editor: *Marjorie Sanders*
Manuscript Editor: *Lynne Fletcher*
Permissions Editor: *Carline Haga*
Interior and Cover Design: *Flora Pomeroy*
Art Coordinator: *Lisa Torri*
Interior Illustration: *Lisa Torri*
Typesetting: *Bookends Typesetting*
Cover Printing: *Phoenix Color Corporation*
Printing and Binding: *Arcata Graphics, Fairfield*

Dedicated to my mother,
Theresa,
who taught me gratitude

Preface

I teach psychology at a large state university in the southeast and also have a private practice in clinical psychology. One day about five years ago, while I was sitting in my easy chair at home, reading a book and thinking about nothing in particular other than the book, my heart rate jumped. This startled me, as I knew of nothing that would account for it. Within seconds, my chest tightened and I was unable to get a full breath. By now, my full attention was on my body as it got progressively more out of control. My face broke out in a cold sweat, I felt disconnected from my environment, I felt light-headed, and my hands and shoulders were tingling. My whole body felt wired.

I was having a panic attack. When I tried to stand up, I felt dizzy and sat back down. The whole experience lasted about an hour. In the months to come, I would have these attacks intermittently, most frequently when I was at rest, with no apparent triggering event. I was familiar with the phenomenon, having treated others for it, so I didn't think I was going crazy, having a heart attack, or beginning to pass out. I did realize that I must be under stress and that it was affecting me more than I had thought.

In the following months I talked with a number of colleagues and students and asked them if they had had similar experiences. A large proportion told me that they had, and most were not troubled by them. My subsequent formal study of panic attacks in "normal" individuals corroborated my informal survey: many people have experienced panic but most have had only transitory episodes and have not been particularly bothered by them.

Further thought made me wonder what differences existed between people who weren't particularly affected by panic attacks and those who began to dread them, avoid situations they associated with them, and, in some cases, develop bizarre methods for coping with them. I recalled one client who would cut his wrists whenever he had a long attack, a coping method that did, in fact, work: his attack would stop after he had cut his wrists.

My personal and professional experience had given me a great deal of information about panic attacks and strategies for coping with them. When I had my first attack, I had already been researching the treatment of panic attacks for a year. My own experience and my growing familiarity with the problem of panic prompted me to reevaluate the approach I'd been using. This book presents the results of that reevaluation. Many case histories are used to illustrate my points. Though based on real people, the histories have been altered to protect the clients' identities.

How to Read This Book

Knowledge is power. Your success in applying what you learn in this book will depend on two things: how much of this information becomes knowledge and how much of that knowledge you put into action. Knowledge can be defined as information that has been experienced and made one's own. If you have been told what it is to love someone, you have information; if you have experienced what it is to love someone, you have knowledge. Obviously, knowledge is much more powerful than information. If you use the information in this book by applying it to your own episodes of panic, you will grow in knowledge; if you do not, all you will have is more information about your problem.

This book presents a straightforward plan to help you deal with your panic attacks and, if relevant, with each phase of your panic disorder. It is designed to help you understand and deal with the factors that predispose you to panic attacks, the symptoms of panic, the cognitions that accompany your panic, and the avoidance patterns that you may develop to deal with them. Even if you don't have panic attacks you will find many of the principles presented here useful in coping with anxiety.

Again, the key to benefiting from this book is using it. Take the time to apply each of the chapters to yourself. In addition to discussing how each of the aspects of panic contributes to your panic attacks, I provide you a way of evaluating each aspect of your problem. If you are using the book to bring about change in your own life, you must assess your present status: the frequency and severity of your panic attacks, what coping strategies you use, and the degree to which you avoid situations you associate with panic. Purchase a small notebook and begin recording this information for a while before instituting any changes. This will enable you to determine how you are progressing as you implement the strategies outlined in the book, as well as whether or not you may need professional help.

This is a practical book: at its heart are step-by-step strategies that will help you cope with your panic in all its aspects. Master as many as you can: the more coping strategies you have at your disposal, the better you will be at overcoming your panic. Like any skill, the more you practice the various strategies and the more automatic they become, the more success you will have in using them. The following guidelines may help you as you apply the strategies to your own problem:

- Don't expect too much when you first start working with strategies. Learning to use coping strategies, like learning to drive a car, is a process. Though your first attempts may be clumsy and arouse anxiety, you will improve with practice.
- Rehearse the strategies thoroughly, first mentally and then in a relatively safe situation. This is similar to practicing driving in a parking lot before going out on the road. You use the strategy but in a situation in which you're least likely to do any damage.
- Pick carefully the first real-life situation in which you will use your strategies. Pick a situation in which failure won't be too painful and in which you are likely to succeed.
- Give yourself credit for simply attempting a new strategy. Though your final goal is to succeed, your first goal is to attempt.
- As you succeed in coping, gradually increase the difficulty of the situation you confront.
- Finally, be prepared for setbacks. There is no such thing as improvement without setbacks. For every two steps forward, you are likely to take one step—and, at times, three steps—back. So be prepared for times when you will be sure that the program you've started is neither working nor going to work, and when you will want to quit the whole program.

One final comment: One of my purposes in writing this book was to enable the reader to become an informed consumer of medical and psychological treatments for panic disorder. Therefore, in the last chapter I summarize the findings about the various medications that are prescribed for panic attacks and the different psychotherapeutic approaches taken in treating panic sufferers. For each medication and psychotherapeutic approach, I discuss the rates of improvement you can reasonably expect, the likely side effects, and the rate at which panic recurs after treatment has ended. This provides you a solid basis for making an informed decision about what treatment to use, or, if you are already using one or more of these treatments, for examining more intelligently their effectiveness in reducing your panic symptoms, anticipatory anxiety, catastrophic thoughts, and avoidance behavior—the various aspects of panic.

Acknowledgments

Many people directly and indirectly encouraged me and nourished me through the writing of this book. Included are my wife, Carolyn

Pickett, and my children, Gretchen and Christina. My clients, especially those with panic disorder, frequently rekindled my enthusiasm with their interest in this endeavor. In addition, Nancy Chapman provided valuable editorial assistance, and Cindy Koziol gave generously of both her encouragement and her time.

My thanks also go to my students who worked on the panic disorder project, contributing ideas, energy, and enthusiasm. They include especially Janet Borden, Susan Broyles, Patti Lou Watkins, and John Hayes. The ideas may have taken root in my own mind, but they blossomed and flowered in interactions with my clients and students. To both of these groups I am very grateful.

In addition, I appreciate the many constructive comments and criticisms made at various stages of this work. Many thanks to the manuscript reviewers: David H. Barlow, State University of New York, Albany; Robert G. Meyer, University of Louisville; and John R. Walker, University of Manitoba.

George A. Clum

Contents

What Is Panic?

At some time in our lives, all of us have experienced panic in relation to some frightening event. Only after such an event is over can you take stock of the experience and examine your reaction. When you panic, your body responds immediately and without conscious thought to prepare you for fight or flight. After your panic subsides, however, you may be able to identify some of the bodily changes you experienced: quickened heart rate, difficulty breathing, increased muscle tension, temporary paralysis perhaps, and, certainly, heightened awareness.

This type of panic originates in response to a recognizable event and therefore makes sense to you. Less clear in their dynamics, but still recognizable causes of panic are the numerous fears and phobias to which many people are susceptible. Conditions that may trigger such fears include loud noises, closed-in spaces, the sight of blood, heights, or speaking to a group of people. If you experience such fears, you may wonder why you have been singled out to suffer such indignities, but you are not bewildered when, encountering the object of your fear, you find your palms sweating, heart racing, and knees knocking. In such encounters, you generally perceive the gradual increase in your symptoms and can usually describe in great detail the changes in your body as you near whatever you fear. Because your fear is related to a specific event or situation, you can usually explain it to yourself, and thus reassure yourself.

But what if your terror had no discernible cause? What if you had no explanation for the terror you were feeling? What if your body felt totally out of control, and all you were doing was sitting in an easy chair?

A Case History

Only recently has the term *panic* been applied to such an experience. Many panic attacks come from "out of the blue"; others occur in situations in which the person feels out of control or trapped by circumstances. People frequently panic in store checkout lines, in restaurants, and on public transportation, for example. Listen to how one woman—Celeste—who had her first attacks while flying, described her experience.

> The panic came as a strong surge through my body and mind and initially was brief but with each episode became longer or came in increasingly rapid rushes. I felt attacked, as though these feelings were coming from somewhere else and were seeking me out. They invaded with such force that I would jump as if jolted out of a sound sleep. My heart pounded so fast and loudly that my chest hurt; my face and hands were clammy and tingly, then hot and sweaty as if in burning fever; all my muscles tensed hard, and I forgot to breathe, pulling in air only in desperate gasps. Bright lights flashed in unison with my heartbeat, and movement outside of me appeared jerky, almost like crude pantomime. "What's happening?" I thought. "The pressure, the noise—my head will burst. Something must be wrong on this plane—surely everyone else knows it." I clutched the chair arms, hoping for some stability and to be able to hold my body together, for I was beginning to feel that I wasn't a part of the scene, that I was disintegrating from my terror, pounding heart, and swirling head. I tried to see if others around me were affected by these forces, but they all appeared calm. Their calmness did little to diminish my terror, only serving to humiliate me into silence. "*I* must be the freak," I thought.
>
> "Stop—why won't this stop? I have to get out of here. But there's no way. I'm locked inside an airplane, floating high above the ground. And there's nothing I can do about it. I'm trapped and alone. Everyone else is okay." I tried internal coaching as a way of calming down, and sometimes it worked. But the panic would return, and "permanent" relief came only when I was safely off the plane and out of the airport. It was this way every time; the only difference was in how long the attacks lasted. Longer and longer each time, it seemed.
>
> I began to feel that I was jeopardizing the lives of others because of how desperate I became in wanting to escape the plane, the reason for my panic. I was convinced that I would cause the plane to crash through some foolish act designed to stop my fear. Throughout it all, though, I made a great effort to hide this terror and desperation, thinking that hiding it would keep it from graduating to hysteria and would make it less fatal. Hysteria, I thought, could only be permanent.

Celeste's experiences typify panic attacks in several respects:

1. She experiences feelings—heart racing, chest pain, feeling hot and sweaty—typical of a panic attack.
2. She has horrifying thoughts that arise from these feelings—"my head will burst," and "I was disintegrating from terror"— thoughts that are also characteristic of panic attacks.
3. She feels trapped in the plane and relieved to be on the ground again.

4. She fears losing control and doing something that would jeopardize everyone on the airplane.

Unlike my own first attack, which I described in the preface, Celeste's first full fledged panic attack came only after a gradual increase in her anxiety level.

> At first I was just easily startled by the foreign sensation of airplane travel. A sudden drop in altitude—my heart would thud, dropping to my stomach, and I was stunned by dizziness. "Understandable," I'd tell myself. But I dreaded the next startling event and the swift fear that would follow. I waited for it. Then at some point my hypersensitivity and dread must have become stronger than any understanding I strived for, and startling events were no longer required. I would panic anyway, usually without any warning, though I was always tensely alert.

People who have specific phobias, which may include fear of animals, heights, or closed spaces, will notice a similarity between their own bodily responses when they encounter whatever they fear and those characterizing a panic attack. Though panic and phobias trigger the same bodily responses, however, and are similarly overwhelming experiences, in the case of panic, no actual threat or fearful condition exists to help explain why your body is responding as it is. Under such circumstances, you are likely to seek out an explanation for your body's response. The explanation you arrive at may either reduce your physical symptoms or increase them even further. If you think you're about to go insane, your symptoms will rapidly worsen, but if you explain to yourself that you've had a very stressful week, your symptoms will likely ease a bit.

Do You Have Panic Attacks?

Symptoms of anxiety are classified as a panic attack when the symptoms occur in sufficient quantity and arise suddenly and without warning. Panic attacks may occur spontaneously—at random—or they may tend to recur in particular situations. They always involve a number of intense symptoms of anxiety that come on suddenly, and they are often accompanied by thoughts of catastrophe. In the revised third edition of the *Diagnostic and Statistical Manual of Mental Disorders* (DSM-III-R), published in 1987 by the American Psychiatric Association, anxiety episodes are defined as panic attacks when at least four spontaneous symptoms are present. Further, persons who have had at least four such episodes of panic within a four-week period are considered to suffer from a panic disorder.

There is no magic to these numbers; they simply represent a convention established to help professionals decide whether or not a person's symptoms are present in sufficient quantity and frequency to warrant concern and perhaps treatment. Please recognize that these numbers are arbitrary. You may consider yourself to have a treatable problem after one brief episode, while someone else might consider several attacks a week no matter of concern. You are the final judge as to whether or not your panic episodes warrant treatment.

The DSM-III-R lists the following as symptoms of a panic attack:

1. shortness of breath or smothering sensation;
2. dizziness, unsteady feelings, or faintness;
3. palpitations or accelerated heart rate;
4. trembling or shaking;
5. sweating;
6. choking;
7. nausea or abdominal distress;
8. depersonalization—feeling that your own body is unreal—or derealization—feeling that your environment is not real;
9. numbness or tingling sensations in one or more parts of your body;
10. hot flashes or chills;
11. chest pain or discomfort;
12. fear of dying; and
13. fear of going crazy or losing self-control.

Remember, experiencing any four of these symptoms during one episode is the primary criterion for diagnosing a panic attack.

This list of panic attack symptoms includes two basic types: bodily changes and thoughts interpreting these changes. As you can see, all of the physical symptoms are associated with increased arousal. When you wake up, for example, your heart rate and respiration also increase but the changes are so gradual and so minute that you are usually unaware of them. During a panic attack, the changes are rapid and dramatic and, because of their severity, quite uncomfortable.

According to the DSM-III-R, one requirement for diagnosing a panic attack is that at least four of the symptoms must have occurred within ten minutes of the appearance of the first symptom. When you have a panic attack, you are aware of a sudden increase in physical discomfort. Your heart rate can increase 50 beats or more per minute within seconds, accompanied by rapid changes in your respiration and body temperature. This suddenness is particularly disturbing and frightening because nothing seems to account for it. No other type of anxiety comes on as dramatically as panic or involves so much of the person.

As we have already seen, panic attacks also lack a clear causal event. Asked to identify what could account for so dramatic a physiological change, most sufferers cannot. This inability to account for what is happening is what leads to the terror expressed in panic sufferers' catastrophic thoughts.

To summarize, you have had a diagnosable panic attack if:

1. You had at least four of the symptoms listed.
2. All four symptoms occurred within ten minutes of the onset of the first symptom.
3. The attack was not associated with a specific object or situation and did not represent an actual threat to your physical well-being.

Let's look at two brief examples that illustrate different aspects of panic attacks.

Case 1

Martin came to see me shortly after his first attack. Three days previously he had begun having episodes at work during which he would feel very hot and would sweat profusely. He reported losing ten pounds in the course of the three days. Though sweating was the chief manifestation of Martin's attacks, he also felt weak, faint, and nauseated. He was afraid the attacks meant that he was going crazy. The episodes came on rapidly within minutes of his walking into his place of employment and then occurred intermittently throughout the day.

Case 2

Martha was referred to me by her physician after she reported an episode in which she awakened from a sound sleep in a state of panic. She reported that during this episode she was gasping for breath, felt her heart beating very fast, and felt dissociated from her environment. She was immediately afraid that she was having a heart attack.

In each of these examples, the individual's symptoms occurred very quickly. Both were spontaneous, in that no situation could be said to have caused them. Though Martin's attacks occurred while he was at work, he did not fear being at work, nor were his attacks caused by any such fear.

From the information given, we can conclude that Martin not only had panic attacks, he also had a panic disorder. Martha, on the other hand, did not have a panic disorder when she entered therapy.

Do You Have a Panic Disorder?

You can have panic attacks and not have a panic disorder. How? Having a panic disorder differs from having panic attacks in one or both of two ways: either you have four attacks in a four-week period, or after one of your attacks, for at least a month, you life in fear of having another attack. Further, to warrant a diagnosis of panic disorder, your panic attacks cannot have been caused by a physical disorder such as amphetamine abuse, caffeine abuse, or hyperthyroidism.

Having a panic disorder is considered to be more severe than simply having panic attacks. Clearly, there is a difference in degree between the two in terms of the frequency with which the panic attacks occur. There is also a second difference: panic disorder reflects a generalized anticipatory fear, a fear of having another attack. You may, of course, experience both frequent attacks and a fear of further attacks. Some people who report both also say that having a panic attack is the only thing that stops them from fearing an attack. Paradoxically, for these people, an attack is therefore comforting as well as fearful.

Panic Disorder with Agoraphobia

Many people who have panic attacks also avoid situations that they associate with panic—situations in which escape might be difficult or help not available in the event of a panic attack. A person exhibiting such avoidance behavior is diagnosed as having agoraphobia. Panic attacks can occur at any time, in any place, and people who have panic attacks often associate them with the place in which they occur. If you have a panic attack in church, for example, you may attribute the attack to being in church and may therefore decide to avoid going. Any situation in which panic attacks occur may become the object of avoidance. Let's listen to Celeste's description of how her pattern of avoidance developed:

> Throughout the eight years that I had these attacks on airplanes, I never sought help in dealing with them, nor did I confide in anyone. Surely it wasn't a problem severe enough to merit anyone's attention but mine, I thought. So I arrived at my own solution. I stopped traveling in airplanes. Simple fear of flying, easy solution. End of panic. That was twelve years ago.
>
> Several months after my final plane trip, I moved from a metropolitan area to a rural area in a different part of the state. This change in lifestyle dictated that I spend more time in my car. Yet I had to drive no farther than fifteen miles to get anywhere that I really needed to go. My most distant destination was a group psychotherapy session held for four hours one evening a week. I had become involved in this group as treatment for depression, and regular attendance was highly important to me.
>
> I was astounded when I began panicking while driving to and from these evening sessions. I thought I'd left that panic in the last airplane. But I couldn't ignore it; the pattern was the same. Again, at first, I had brief but powerful surges of panic that jolted me in my seat as if I were startled by something—"maybe it was taking that last curve too fast," I would think, "or being blinded by headlights, or catching sight of that car racing up behind me—what, what, what? This can't be happening again. It can't.

Please stop. Stop!" The surge often was replaced by visible shaking that had begun deep inside of me. I would grip the steering wheel so that I could stay on the road, stay in my seat, and stay on the ground. I envisioned myself as being thrown around inside the car, and since I was no longer in control of the car, it would swerve all over the road and embankments. I was a menace on the road.

I sought explanations, none of which were convincing. The trips to and from group therapy became a nightmare, and I dreaded the approach of each meeting day. I felt incapable of driving the route I needed to take and of driving in the dark. After a year, I stopped attending the weekly sessions. That decision was motivated primarily by reasons other than my growing panic, but I was happy to be free of the predictable weekly panic. I had never once mentioned my panic to the group. "I should be able to solve it," I figured. "It can't be too important because no one else seems to have a problem like this. It's trivial."

But the panic continued even without my weekly thirty-mile round trips in the dark, and I was less able to convince myself that it was trivial. It consumed more and more of my energy and self-esteem. I avoided driving or riding in cars at night, but my panic had ceased being a nighttime phenomenon. I could no longer predict when I would feel the terror and confusion of another attack.

I was then driving nine miles to work, half of that distance on a divided, four-lane highway. That stretch of road became a major obstacle to my getting to or from my office. One morning I pulled off that section four times because I was terrified at my panic and thought that it would surely lead me to kill myself and every other driver. I knew I was incapable of driving on that road. "High speeds and other cars—that's the problem," I decided. So I found another route on back roads with lower speed limits and far less traffic. Unfortunately, it was virtually impassable in winter. I moved closer to my office, within walking distance, actually. I still felt relatively safe driving within the town limits at speeds of twenty-five and thirty-five miles per hour, but I was relieved that now I wouldn't be forced to drive to work or the grocery store. But now the panic wasn't just in cars. The now-familiar beginning twinges of panic happened in other situations—in stores, at restaurants, at home. I did my best to ignore them.

I searched for a way to be able to continue my activities even if the panic should occur. I found that I could sometimes handle what was happening by creating a visual tunnel that allowed me to block out everything that I thought was scaring me, everything external to me and the path upon which I had to travel. My eyes set fast on a goal ahead of me, I could progress in stages, from one visual goal to the next. If I decreased my speed of travel as I reduced my visual world, I felt even safer because I had more control in a less complicated environment. I did this with two results: I could reach my set goal (which might be the next place to pull off the road or might mean driving yet another mile) and so felt victorious. But I was also sickened later when I realized that I had been operating a car unaware of what was occurring around me. I wondered if in the future I would simply shut my eyes tightly so as not to see anything around me, if everything began to scare me.

Obviously, out-of-town visits to family and friends became infrequent, as did shopping and recreation that required my leaving the town limits. I had a reputation of being "tense" in cars and various other situations, but again I let no one know the real reason I was curtailing my travel and activities. I still tried to appear composed, which was difficult, so I stayed close to home. That was the easiest solution, just like not flying. I was well aware that my fears about panicking had made my life a solitary one, but it seemed a necessary trade-off for keeping the fears away.

As you can see, though Celeste began by avoiding only one situation, she ended up avoiding many. Avoiding situations you associate with panic presents a major complication in the treatment of panic—a complication we will examine in detail later on. At this point, it is important only to note that people often respond to panic by avoiding situations and that such avoidance presents additional problems in the treatment of panic.

Panic Attacks and Other Anxiety Disorders

Panic attacks differ from simple and social phobias in three ways:

1. Panic attacks are unpredictable, whereas simple and social phobias are always associated with specific situations.
2. Your cognitive interpretations of what is happening to you during a panic attack are extreme: you believe you are dying or going crazy. In simple and social phobias, you can attribute your symptoms to your presence in the situation.
3. Simple and social phobias are avoidable: you can manage to stay away from escalators or tall buildings if they are what you fear. Even if you avoid situations in which you have had panic attacks, however, you are likely to experience other attacks in situations that are unavoidable—in your own home, for instance.

The basic difference between panic attacks and simple phobias is in what evokes the anxiety. Though a person who has simple phobias can experience anxiety of panic proportions if suddenly placed in the situation he or she fears, *it is being in the situation that triggers the panic.* People who experience panic attacks may avoid specific situations, but it is not fear of the situations themselves that provokes their panic attacks.

Three differences also distinguish panic attacks from general anxiety:

1. General anxiety does not involve the extreme physical changes that characterize panic attacks. Because of this, general anxiety is usually experienced as more uncomfortable than frightening.

2. General anxiety is associated with milder types of thoughts: worry or vague discomfort. Panic attacks, in contrast, are accompanied by thoughts of catastrophe.
3. General anxiety is more of a chronic condition: you feel anxious all the time. Panic attacks come and go and are relatively brief: intense anxiety is followed by a period of relative calm.

Are Panic Attacks and Panic Disorders Common?

Most victims of panic attacks believe that they are the only persons in the world—or certainly among the few—to suffer such an affliction. They are startled to find that as many as one out of every three adults has had a panic attack in the last year. That's right! Researchers in one study, examining the incidence of infrequent panic attacks, found that 33% of those asked reported at least one attack in the last year.[1] Furthermore, it has been shown that 80% of individuals with anxiety-related diagnoses such as simple phobias, social phobias, and generalized anxiety disorder also experience panic attacks. Even if we consider only those people who have a panic disorder, we're still talking about 2% of the population—more than 4 million people in the United States alone. And though this is a considerable number, it is likely an underestimate for two reasons.

First, the primary symptoms of a panic attack are physical, not psychological, so many sufferers seek out a physician rather than a psychologist. Many people seek psychological treatment of panic only after they have consulted a series of physicians, including internists, cardiologists, and surgeons. Further, because they view their problem as a physical one, panic sufferers are less likely to recognize the possibility that it might be psychological. Asked if they experience panic attacks, such people may respond in the negative, unaware that their symptoms are a severe form of acute anxiety.

Second, the 2% figure is based on an outdated definition of panic disorder. The old definition required three panic attacks within a three-week period before a diagnosis was warranted. The current definition requires only a single panic attack when it is followed by a month of anticipating further attacks. This more liberal definition will lead to an increase in the number of people identified as having a panic disorder.

Clearly, panic attacks are not rare: as many as one out of every three adults has had at least one in the past year. Clearly, neither are panic

---

[1]Norton, G. R., Harrison, B., Hauch, J., & Rhodes, L. (1985). Characteristics of people with infrequent panic attacks. *Journal of Abnormal Psychology, 94,* 216–221.

disorders: approximately 4.5 million people in the United States will have such a disorder in their lifetime. This last estimate, further, is almost certainly an underestimate. Regardless of the precise numbers, one conclusion is inescapable: you are not alone with your problem!

The Stages of a Panic Attack

Panic attacks can be shown to go through several stages, including:

1. a *preparatory stage* preceding the onset of panic attacks;
2. an acute stage, during which a panic attack is occurring;
3. an *appraisal stage,* coinciding with and following attacks, during which you try to understand your attacks;
4. an *intensification stage,* which occurs if your appraisal triggers an increase in your symtoms; or a *resolution stage,* which occurs if your appraisal triggers a decrease in your symptoms; and
5. a *residual stage,* corresponding to the period of exhaustion that follows an attack.

Though panic attacks appear to come out of the blue, in fact, they develop out of a background of psychological stress. In some people, this stress results in greater anxiety, while in others, the stress causes deeper depression. Oftentimes there is a gradual, even imperceptible increase in stress. This stage, which lays the basis for panic attacks, I have called the preparatory stage. It is characterized by high levels of chronic stress such as you would experience in a high-stress job or conflict-laden marriage. In this stage, you are filled with anxiety as you attempt to resolve your conflicts or reduce your stress but view all alternatives as negative. You thus perceive your situation to be inescapable and feel trapped within it. Though a number of people who go through such conflicts never develop panic attacks, those people who have panic attacks have gone through such a preparatory stage. This stage prepares the ground for the second stage, in which panic attacks emerge.

The second stage is the acute stage. It is characterized by the sudden, seemingly inexplicable eruption of panic attacks. If you examine the events immediately preceding your panic attacks, you may paradoxically find that you were in a period of relatively low stress when they first occurred. Upon closer examination, however, you will always find that a high-stress period preceded the low-stress period. You seem to be recovering from the high stress when the first panic attack erupts. This attack occurs suddenly and without warning.

Because of the intensity of the experience and the difficulty of identifying a clear causal agent, you enter the third stage.

This is the appraisal stage of a panic attack. In this stage, you search for explanations of this event. You scan your immediate and previous environment for information to help explain the attack. Depending on your ability to come up with a reasonable explanation, you will enter either the intensification stage or the resolution stage.

If you cannot explain the symptoms of your panic attack in terms that relate the attack to stressful, conflict-laden events in your life, you enter the intensification stage. You then shift, in your cognitive appraisal, toward catastrophic explanations for what is happening to you. If you believe that you may be experiencing a stroke, heart attack, or other physical ailment, you may immediately call the rescue squad or go to the nearest hospital's emergency room. On the other hand, if you attribute your experience to your being under a lot of stress, you are likely to find this explanation reasonable and enter a resolution stage. In this stage, you reassure yourself that all is understandable and that you will be able to regain control. In essence, if your cognitive appraisal is catastrophic, your symptoms are sure to intensify before they subside. If your appraisal is rational and reassuring, your symptoms will gradually subside.

Regardless of the outcome of your appraisal, the symptoms of the acute stage will eventually subside. Some of your symptoms may persist at a lower level; some may be replaced by other symptoms, such as extreme fatigue or weakness. This stage, the residual stage of your panic attack, represents the effect on the body of a prolonged period of arousal. This arousal depletes some of the body's stored energy, causing fatigue. Those who have felt this fatigue report that it is unlike any other fatigue they have experienced. They describe feeling as though every nerve fiber has been exhausted and they have been left drained without having exerted themselves. This stage of a panic attack adds to your feeling of demoralization because you have less energy left to withstand stress.

The Anticipatory Response

Panic attacks become panic disorder, with or without agoraphobia, when you begin to dread the onset of the next attack. From your own experience, you know that panic attacks are extremely unpleasant. Consequently, coming to anticipate future attacks is the next development in the progression. At this stage, which really occurs between attacks, you are likely to find yourself becoming increasingly vigilant in examining your body for signs that an attack is about to occur. You

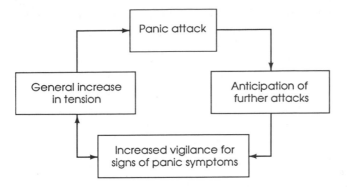

Figure 1.1 The anticipatory response

may begin interpreting even normal increases in your heart rate or breathing rate, such as occur during exercise or when climbing a flight of stairs, as indications of an ensuing attack. It is easy to see that this stage brings with it an increase in your overall level of tension, which in turn increases your chances of having additional attacks.

Once you enter this stage, both the frequency and duration of your attacks increase. This stage has also been called "the fear of fear response." There are many reasons to fear fear. Being afraid feels bad, is embarrassing, and means a temporary loss of control that may cause you to behave unpredictably, with possibly disastrous consequences. This fear of fear can become so powerful that it dominates your life, coloring all of your behavior and controlling even your thoughts.

One of my clients, a woman named Suzie, began anticipating attacks so intensely that the anticipation and waiting became worse than her actual attacks. When she then had a panic attack, it only served to make her feel that her anticipation was justified. She even experienced a sense of relief at having an attack and was able for a short while to stop anticipating one. Of course, this respite was brief, and soon she was again scanning her body for symptoms.

The Avoidance Response

Constantly anticipating panic attacks often increases the likelihood that you will begin avoiding places and situations in which you have had panic attacks in the past. Though not all people who have panic attacks avoid specific places, a large number do. Let's examine more closely the connection between anticipating an attack and avoidance.

Panic attacks, when frequent, occur in a pattern. You may tend to have them when you are in crowds, while alone, when resting after a tough week, or during sleep. Regardless of where or in what circumstances your attacks may occur, anticipating their arrival involves not only scanning your body for evidence of their onset but also examining your environment for any patterns into which they might fall. Once you think you have identified a pattern, two things occur: (1) You become more vigilant for signs of a panic attack when you are in that situation, and (2) Your level of tension increases prior to entering and while you are in that situation.

This increase in tension further increases your chances of having a panic attack, creating a self-fulfilling prophecy. Your fear of an attack triggers one. And once you have identified certain situations as "high risk," it is a short step to avoiding those situations. The reasoning is simple: if I go to that restaurant, I'm more likely to have a panic attack; therefore, I won't go to that restaurant, and I won't have a panic attack. The reasoning seems sound. The only problem with it is *it's wrong*! Choosing to limit the situations you will enter leads down an increasingly life-constricting path. It is, rather, the avoidance response that we must avoid. Because of the importance of the avoidance response and its disruptive effects on people's lives, we will consider it and its treatment in greater detail in later chapters.

Is It Panic Without Panicky Thoughts?

Our definition of panic lists the fears of dying and going crazy or losing control as just two of the symptoms that contribute to a diagnosis of a panic attack. But what if the other symptoms occur and yet you perceive yourself to be in no particular danger? If you had a rapid pulse, tight chest, lump in your throat, and rapid breathing and you were riding a roller coaster, then you would consider yourself excited. In such an instance, you would have no trouble in concluding that no panic attack had occurred. Yet you experienced four symptoms of panic. What if there were no roller coaster to explain your physiological symptoms but you still felt no concern? Should your symptoms still be diagnosed as indicating a panic attack? In my opinion, as well as that of many other professionals, they should not.

Two researchers—Stanley Schachter and Jerome Singer—conducted a study to learn what part a person's situation plays in determining what emotions he or she feels.[2] Volunteers were injected with adrenaline, a substance that produces arousal symptoms similar to but not as severe as those of panic. The volunteers were then divided into four

[2]Schachter, S., & Singer, J. E. (1962). Cognitive, social and physiological determinants of emotional state. *Psychological Review, 69,* 379–399.

groups. Two of the groups were told what effects to expect from the adrenaline injection, while the other two were told nothing of its effects. While "waiting for the experiment to begin," each of the four groups encountered in the waiting room an individual who had been instructed to act either happy or angry. The research conditions and results are summarized in Figure 1.2.

When they asked the volunteers to report their emotions, Schachter and Singer found some interesting results. The volunteers who had been told the effects of the injection were not affected by the encounter in the waiting room. Those who had not been told the effects of the injection were affected. Those who had encountered the angry person were more likely to report feeling angry, while those who encountered the happy person were more likely to report feeling happy.

One of the more important conclusions to come out of this study is that a person's physiological state does not solely determine his or her emotions. Though all the study's participants were physiologically aroused, the circumstances in which they were placed had an important role in determining their emotions. This is similar to the example given earlier of someone riding a roller coaster and interpreting his or her physiological changes as indicating excitement rather than panic.

What do we make of the finding in this experiment that only the volunteers who did not know the effects of the injection were affected by the encounter in the waiting room? Since everyone in the study experienced an increase in arousal, we can assume that everyone was faced with the need to explain this increased arousal—in other words, to attribute it to something. Psychologists call this phenomenon *attribution.* Individuals who were told the effects of the drug could attribute their arousal to the drug. Those who were not told had to

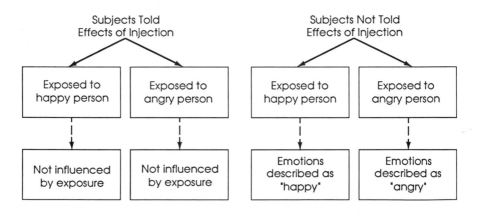

Figure 1.2 The conditions and results of Schachter and Singer's experiment

search elsewhere for an explanation and were more likely to look to their environment for cues to help them explain it. These people were thus more influenced by their waiting room experience, interpreting their arousal according to the external cues they received.

How does this study contribute to our understanding of panic? Consider again what happens in a panic attack. You have a sudden, unexplainable increase in your level of arousal that prepares you for fight or flight. Faced with such an occurrence, you have a natural and probably intense need to explain what is happening, using whatever cues are available. If you have recently experienced a major loss, such as death of a loved one, divorce, or loss of a job, you may well conclude, "I have been under a great deal of stress lately, and this is my body's response to it." On the other hand, if you have not experienced any significant recent stress, you may look further for a possible explanation. If your father died of a heart attack at the age of 48, and you are now approaching this age, you may well reason, "My father died of a heart attack at a young age. I am genetically vulnerable to heart attacks. Chest pain is a symptom of a heart attack. I'M HAVING A HEART ATTACK!"

As Schachter and Singer's study showed, in the absence of accurate and adequate information, you will use the most obvious data you have at your disposal to explain what you are feeling. Given an adequate explanation such as "I've been injected with adrenaline and it accounts for my arousal," or "I've been under stress and that is why my body is responding this way," you are unlikely to panic. Rather, you are most likely to panic when experiencing a strong physiological response in a situation where there are few cues to explain your response.

Summary

Let's summarize the principal characteristics of panic attacks, panic disorder, and panic disorder with agoraphobia.

1. Panic attacks are sudden, dramatic increases in arousal.
2. Panic attacks often arise spontaneously in no particular situation, though you may later identify a pattern of situations in which they are more likely to occur.
3. Panic attacks are accompanied by catastrophic imaginings of what might happen during or as the result of the attack.
4. When panic attacks occur frequently or you find yourself anticipating further attacks, a diagnosis of panic disorder is warranted.
5. Once you begin anticipating panic attacks, the frequency and severity of your attacks are likely to increase. This is a natural

result of the increase in your overall level of tension caused by your anticipation and by hypervigilance in looking for signs that you are about to have an attack. At this level of severity, anticipation frequently leads to avoidance behavior.

6. If you begin avoiding situations that you associate with panic attacks, you have a disorder known as panic disorder with agoraphobia.

7. Your appraisal of what is causing your feelings is called attribution. What you attribute your symptoms to is essential in determining the severity and duration of your attacks.

2

What Causes Panic?

People who suffer chronic panic attacks often think that they are the only ones in the world to endure such a fate. They look around at their friends and wonder why they experience severe anxiety in situations their friends seem to handle with ease. This view is myopic, for, as we have seen, a large percentage of the population has occasional panic attacks, though not necessarily with the frequency or with the attendant catastrophic thoughts experienced by a much smaller percentage of the population. In this chapter, we will address a number of questions: (1) Why do panic attacks develop at all? (2) Why do they become burdensome or even debilitating for 2% of the population? (3) Are some people predisposed to panic attacks, and if so, is their predisposition physiological, genetic, or learned? (4) Does stress play a part? Must it be chronic stress, catastrophic stress, or stress of some other kind? (5) Do people who experience an occasional attack but who do not develop a full-fledged disorder think about their attacks or cope with them differently than those for whom panic attacks become a chronic and debilitating problem?

A Causal Model

To answer these questions, I have developed a model that illustrates how panic attacks develop. This model is presented in Figure 2.1. Let's examine this figure. Two levels of consciousness are represented: there are conscious factors, of which we are aware, and unconscious factors, or factors outside of our awareness. Notice that the factors that precede a panic attack—Level A in the figure—are largely outside of our awareness. These include any genetic predispositions, which lead to physiological vulnerabilities, and environmental events that lead to psychological vulnerabilities. Some or all of these may combine to increase your vulnerability to a panic attack.

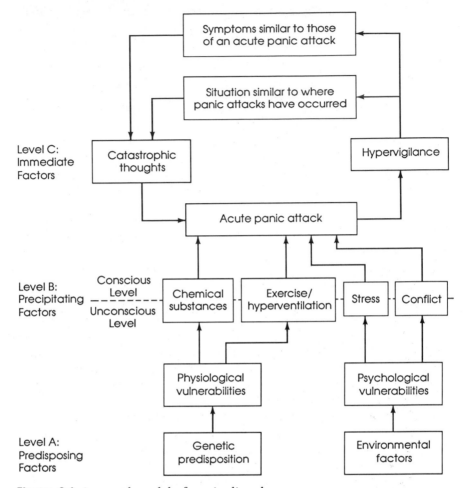

Figure 2.1 A causal model of panic disorders

   The more predisposing factors that are present, the greater is your vulnerability to developing panic attacks. You may or may not develop panic attacks, however, even if you possess all of these predisposing factors.

   At the next level in the development of panic disorders—Level B in Figure 2.1—are the precipitating factors, those factors that lead most immediately to the development of panic. These factors are shown as straddling the line between the conscious and the unconscious, because though you may be aware of the factors themselves, you are probably not aware of their connection to panic attacks. Chemical precipitants include such things as excessive caffeine or alcohol intake. Hyperventilation (excessively rapid breathing), or increased sodium lactate in your body produced by vigorous exercise or chronic muscle tension also act as precipitants. Psychological factors that can trigger panic include conflicts with others or within yourself and acute or chronic stress.

Once the first panic attack has occurred—Level C—it is capable of taking on a life of its own. The attack occurs on a conscious level, in that you are aware of your symptoms, thoughts, and circumstances. Once an attack has occurred, the vulnerabilities and precipitants that contributed to the first panic attack are no longer necessary to produce further attacks. The attack itself is a powerful learning experience. Terrified during the attack, you become hypervigilant. You look for, and find, signs that another attack is about to begin. You may find such signs in symptoms similar to those of panic, in the thoughts that accompany panic, or in situations that you associate with panic. Being an inventive human being, you are capable of finding signs of an impending attack in facts only remotely connected to your attacks.

Your preoccupation with the changes occurring in your body increases your overall levels of depression and anxiety, emotional states that further increase the likelihood of additional attacks. Previously neutral situations such as driving, being home alone, and being in public places take on an aura of menace because you begin to perceive them as circumstances in which an attack may occur. Previously neutral changes in your body—an increase in your heart rate after climbing a flight of stairs or feeling light-headed after rising suddenly from a reclining position—frighten you into thinking that a full-fledged panic attack may follow shortly.

This chapter will focus on the factors that underlie panic attacks, most of which exist on the unconscious level. We will also examine precipitating factors, leaving an analysis of the factors that operate during an attack to later chapters. Let's now examine each of the predisposing factors more closely.

Biological Factors

Genetic Predisposition

Researchers use a variety of methods to determine whether or not a genetic predisposition to an illness may exist, chiefly by studying how often that illness occurs in identical and fraternal twins, both those reared together and those reared apart. If identical twins develop the illness much more often than fraternal twins, researchers can conclude that some genetic predisposition does exist, since identical twins are twice as similar to each other, genetically speaking, as fraternal twins are. Likewise, if identical twins that were reared apart from birth develop the illness much more often than people in the general population, researchers can conclude the same thing, since twins raised apart are affected by the environment to the same degree as any other pair of people chosen from the general population. If the illness tends to run in families, a genetic predisposition may also exist.

Panic disorder does tend to run in families: though only 2% of the general population has a panic disorder, among the immediate family members of panic attack sufferers the rate is 15%. This is far from conclusive evidence of a genetic predisposition, however, because panic may be learned rather than inherited. Children may learn to panic directly, by watching a parent have an anxiety attack, or indirectly, by hearing constant warnings to avoid situations in which one might get lost or confused. Nevertheless, it has been my experience, as well as that of other researchers, that panic disorders frequently run in families and that some genetic predisposition to panic attacks may indeed exist.

What does it mean to be predisposed to developing panic disorders? It means that you are more likely to experience panic attacks in response to less stress than individuals who are not predisposed. This predisposition, if it is genetic, exists in fewer than half of those people who develop panic disorders. What of the majority of people for whom there is no evidence of a genetic predisposition to panic disorder? Their panic disorder may result from a learned vulnerability or perhaps from severe or prolonged stress.

There are several reasons for concluding that panic disorders are only minimally related to a genetic predisposition. First, the evidence that supports a genetic predisposition is weak, being based solely on the rates of occurrence of the disorder in families. The same data could also be interpreted as supporting learned anxiety responses. Second, as we have seen, a large percentage of the general population has at least one panic attack per year. Since only 2% of the population has panic disorder, it is highly unlikely that such a large segment of the population would have what might be termed a mild genetic predisposition. Third, even individuals who develop frequent panic attacks have periods without attacks. For people with a genetic predisposition to panic, factors other than genetics must be playing a more central role to produce the waxing and waning of symptoms.

Can those who suffer panic attacks determine if and to what degree they are genetically predisposed? Though there is no direct test for determining genetic predisposition, you can estimate it by first determining if and how many members of your immediate family have a panic disorder and how severe their disorder has been. Divide the number of members who have a panic disorder by the total number of people in your immediate family and multiply by 100 to arrive at a percentage. If more than 15% of them have the disorder (the rate shown by research to be characteristic among family members), the chances of your having a genetic predisposition increase.

A second step is to assess whether or not you might have learned to panic. For example, if one or both of your parents have had frequent panic attacks but you have never seen them have an attack and they have never discussed them with you, then your panic attacks can probably not be attributed to your having learned such responses from your parents. The chances of your having a genetic predisposition accordingly increase.

A third step is to assess your level of stress before the onset of your panic. If the stress was severe, prolonged, or related to an unresolvable problem, then you are less likely to have a genetic predisposition. If, on the other hand, you experienced minimal or no stress preceding your attacks, then the likelihood again increases.

Physiological and Chemical Factors

Sodium Lactate. Some consider panic disorder to be caused entirely by chemical substances in the body. The link between chemical substances and panic disorder has been considered to be so strong, in fact, that some investigators have labeled panic disorder primarily a biological disease. Physiologically speaking, people who develop panic disorders might be considered predisposed to respond to some of these chemicals, exhibiting the excessive anxiety characteristic of panic attacks.

The substance that has attracted the most attention is one that is believed to be central to the development of panic attacks: sodium lactate. The amount of this substance in your body increases in response to physical exertion. If you exercise vigorously one day, the soreness in your muscles the next day is related to increased concentrations of sodium lactate. Early studies found that sodium lactate, when injected into the body, produced panic attacks in people who already had panic attacks but less often produced attacks in people who did not have them. Since the same did not occur when people with panic attacks were injected with a neutral substance such as a salt water solution, the researchers concluded that sodium lactate caused the attacks. Since sodium lactate exists in your body naturally, and since people with panic attacks seemed to be uniquely vulnerable to injected sodium lactate, the researchers further concluded that individuals with panic attacks are physiologically vulnerable to natural increases of sodium lactate in their bodies. Such an increase could be produced by chronic stress or chronic overexertion.

More recent information challenges this conclusion. Sodium lactate has been shown to produce panic attacks in people who are highly anxious, regardless of whether or not they experience panic attacks. People with panic disorders are therefore not uniquely vulnerable to sodium lactate. Further, though sodium lactate may produce an attack when injected in a person who has panic attacks at that point in time, it may fail to do so at another time when the same person is not having attacks. Vulnerability to sodium lactate can thus fluctuate in the same person. Other substances, such as adrenaline, are also capable of triggering an attack in people who are vulnerable— that is, people whose general state of anxiety is already high.

So, what does happen when you receive an injection of sodium lactate or when physical exertion elevates your body's sodium lactate levels? Sodium lactate does produce some symptoms of panic. Since you have learned to associate your fear of attacks with these symptoms, you may respond with catastrophic thoughts, triggering additional symptoms and producing a full-fledged panic attack.

If this is how sodium lactate produces panic, as you become familiar with its physical effects, you should panic less and less. This is, in fact, what happens: with repeated injections, the panic reaction diminishes; the person learns what to expect and how to cope with it. Other research has shown that treatment aimed at improving people's skills in coping with panic also reduces their vulnerability to sodium lactate injections. Such research also suggests that a person's vulnerability to sodium lactate may be largely psychological.

Caffeine. Though sodium lactate occurs naturally in our bodies, other substances that are capable of precipitating panic attacks do not. One of the most common is caffeine. Panic disorder sufferers, especially when experiencing frequent attacks, have a known physiological susceptibility to caffeine. In fact, specific attacks can be directly traced to caffeine intake. Researchers have also demonstrated that ingesting caffeine, even when an individual does not know what he or she is taking, can produce marked symptoms in people with panic.

Alcohol. While alcohol itself is a central nervous system depressant, excessive alcohol consumption is often followed by an increase in somatic arousal. Depending on the amount of alcohol consumed, the drinker may experience increased respiration, jitteriness, elevated heart rates, and cold sweats. In individuals who are having panic attacks, these symptoms may trigger an attack.

Heart Conditions. Not surprisingly, people who have had heart attacks are at risk for developing panic attacks. In addition, mitral valve prolapse syndrome, a usually benign condition that produces subtle cardiac changes diagnosable only with an echocardiogram, has been shown—along with a number of conditions that are not life-threatening—to be associated with an increased likelihood of panic attacks.

Other Physical Conditions. Many other physical conditions are also associated with an increased risk of panic attacks, including asthma, allergic reactions, hyperthyroidism, and inner ear problems. Among the more common physical problems that may make a person more vulnerable to attacks are insomnia, headaches, painful menstruation, colds, diarrhea, and fatigue. Why should all of these conditions be associated with a higher likelihood of developing panic?

All of these conditions produce symptoms that resemble those of panic. Yet most of the individuals who have the problems listed above do not develop panic attacks: clearly, no simple causal relationship exists here. The similarity of symptoms may lead some to interpret these physical conditions as signs of a panic attack; colds and allergies, for example, cause congestion and breathing difficulty, symptoms that can easily lead to a panic attack in a person who is anticipating one.

More likely, however, people who have these, or other, physical conditions worry about their health, becoming hypervigilant in regard to their bodies. This creates a self-perpetuating cycle in which the hypervigilance leads to greater anxiety, greater anxiety leads to heightened symptoms, heightened symptoms lead to greater vigilance, and so on, until the person's anxiety level reaches panic proportions.

Recommendations. Several recommendations follow from this information:

1. You should have a thorough physical to determine the possible relation of medical conditions to your panic attacks.
2. You should eliminate caffeine and reduce your alcohol intake to a minimum.
3. You should recognize that flare-ups in medical conditions may contribute to a worsening of your panic symptoms.

Psychological Factors

Before we look at how specific psychological factors contribute to the development of panic, let's examine several case histories to set the stage for our analysis. Each case presents a different mixture of genetic and psychological factors, to illustrate how you can begin to think about your own background and its role in your panic attacks.

Case 1

Ralph was a 43-year-old man who had experienced severe panic attacks for nine months before consulting me. Further, nine years before, he had been hospitalized because of depression and had been treated with antidepressant medications and, eventually, electroshock. Ralph described his hospitalization in horrific terms, being separated from his family and ignored by his doctors. Most significant was an episode in which he was awake during the beginning of one of his electroshock treatments. He recalled being unable to breathe because of a rubber mouth guard inserted to prevent him from biting his tongue, and fearing he would choke to death. Later panic attacks occurred whenever he experienced any difficulty breathing.

Ralph's panic attacks began with several occurring over a one-week period, the first one while he was at home and subsequent ones at work. He lost considerable sleep worrying over what was happening to him, fearing that he was losing control and would again have to be hospitalized. For economic reasons, he felt unable to leave his job, even to take some time off temporarily, so he continued to suffer through work despite his emotional state. His panic attacks escalated, and by the end of the week he had resigned from his job. Interestingly, Ralph also reported experiencing panic in situations in which he felt trapped, such as in dentists' chairs or restaurants.

Ralph's history included a not-very-happy marriage, which he felt he could not leave because of financial circumstances and a commitment to raising his children. Further, he did not consider himself emotionally fit enough to get by on his own. He related that earlier in his life, when he was in high school, his father had required him to take a job. Because of this job, Ralph's grades slipped, and he eventually dropped out of school before graduating. Ralph described his relationship with his father as very distant and reported feeling as though he was constantly trying to please his father but never succeeding.

Analysis. Ralph likely had a genetic predisposition to panic attacks, inasmuch as his mother, sister, and daughter all had panic attacks but being trapped in a job he didn't like but didn't feel he could leave precipitated his attacks. Ralph was particularly vulnerable to this type of stress because of his father's "trapping" him in a job while he was in high school. The important consideration here is not whether Ralph was in fact trapped but rather that he *perceived* himself to be trapped.

The symptoms of Ralph's attacks were identical to the feelings he'd had when he'd found himself awake at the beginning of the electroshock treatment: difficulty in breathing, rapid heart rate, and the thought that he couldn't breathe. When he found himself trapped in a similar situation, he was likely to have a panic attack. When his first panic attack occurred, Ralph was overwhelmed by its power and his belief that it meant he would soon lapse into insanity, a reminder of his previous hospitalization. He believed that the only difference between his previous hospitalization and the one that he was sure was about to occur was that this time he "would never be released." Certain of the truth of his belief, he interpreted every symptom as a sign of coming disaster, increasing both his terror and his sense of losing control. As sometimes happens in such situations, Ralph responded panic attacks. This only served to reinforce his perception of himself as ill and incapable of coping with his situation.

Case 2

Mary, 36 years old, had experienced panic attacks off and on for six years before we first met. She could identify no precipitant for her attacks, which sometimes lasted up to two days at a time and seemed to occur both at home and at work. As far as she knew, no other member of her family had experienced such attacks, though she described her father as nervous and tense. She had been hospitalized approximately eight years before, with a diagnosis of manic-depressive illness. She was treated with medication but stopped using it shortly after her discharge from the hospital, and she reported no recurrence of severe depression or mania.

On closer analysis, Mary's attacks proved to be associated with several specific situations: (1) being at work, when she was "pressing" hard for an extended period of time; (2) preparing to return to work at the end of a weekend; (3) arguing with her husband; and (4) situations in which she was being evaluated, either by her husband, her three children, or a superior at work. There were some indications that Mary had responded to a series of panic attacks in the past by leaving previous jobs. She had recently learned to distract herself from her symptoms by engaging in a variety of different tasks, such as shopping and doing housework. If her attacks continued to escalate, she would avoid situations she knew to be stressful or contact a physician.

Mary's lifestyle appeared to be the primary source of stress in her life, as she combined two jobs: homemaker and full-time salesperson. She always pushed herself frantically to succeed and, indeed, had succeeded as a salesperson in a number of different positions. She was basically displeased with her career in sales, however, having always wanted to be a physician, a position she had once prepared for but dropped because of poor grades.

Mary described her father as punitive and perfectionistic, a physician whom she could never please and who made her feel guilty whenever she pursued her own interests. Mary eventually adopted her father's standards for herself, working 80-hour weeks to meet those standards. Although she loved her husband, she believed that she was always wrong and he was always right, a perception that led her to resent and verbally attack him, after which she would feel remorse and berate herself with the thought that he was right and she was wrong.

Analysis. Mary's panic attacks appeared to have little to do with a genetic predisposition, as no member of her family had ever had a panic attack. Rather, Mary had learned to drive herself relentlessly and, in doing so, caused herself perpetual stress. The longstanding nature of Mary's attacks underscored the chronicity of the stress and its relationship to her lifestyle. Whenever the stress became acute, as when she was being evaluated, panic attacks were likely. Her methods of coping with her stress—trying to distract herself and pushing herself even harder—succeeded at first but ultimately increased rather than decreased both her stress and the frequency of her attacks.

Case 3

Jean, 38 years old and the mother of two, had developed panic attacks two months before our first meeting, immediately after her husband had left to move in with his lover. An ambivalent relationship with her husband followed in which she both wanted him back and was fiercely angry and wanted him to stay away. After Jean's husband left, her panic attacks frequently followed crises with her children: she would waken in the middle of the night in panic, feeling unable to handle the multiple roles her husband's leaving presented her. Though Jean found the attacks very unpleasant, she did not respond to them with catastrophic thoughts. She resolved her situation quickly when she decided that she did not want her husband back and that she could handle the roles of mother and household manager quite adequately.

Jean's history revealed a woman whose role in her family had been to take charge in a crisis. Even when Jean had been a little girl, family members had seemed to sense her competence and had turned to her. Her husband and children continued this pattern, leaving her essentially no one to turn to in a crisis. Losing her husband threatened her self-concept, but only briefly, as she reverted to her long-standing habit of making decisions and resolving conflicts.

Analysis. There was little reason to believe that Jean had any genetic predisposition, as no other member of her family had experienced panic attacks. Further, Jean's precrisis personality was highly adaptive and allowed her to solve problems readily. An acute stressor, her husband's departure, briefly threatened Jean's sense of competence and probably triggered the panic attacks. Though the stressor continued to exist, she took charge of her own situation, and her attacks stopped.

The above cases illustrate three different avenues by which panic attacks may develop. Though numerous other avenues are possible, I will use these three as a starting point to illustrate the importance of stress, learned vulnerabilities, one's general level of psychological adjustment, how one appraises the experience of panic, and one's style of coping in the development and sustenance of panic attacks. My discussion draws on my own experience and research with individuals who have panic disorder as well as on the research of other investigators.

Stress

Stress is *always* involved in the onset of panic. Sometimes the stress is chronic and has existed for a long time; at other times it is of recent origin. If you ask panic attack sufferers to identify the stressors that preceded the onset of their attacks, they will not always be able to do so. When you begin to explore their lives, however, the connection between stress and panic onset becomes obvious.

Acute Stress. Jean's case illustrates this type of stress. Though Jean's husband's leaving could have led to chronic stress, as might have happened had Jean continued to try to work out a relationship with her husband while he lived with his lover, such events are for the most part transitory.

The Holmes and Rahe Social Readjustment Rating Scale, reproduced in Table 2.1, illustrates the types of acute stressors that have been shown to increase anxiety as well as cause other emotional difficulties. You can use this scale to measure your overall level of stress by calculating your score for each of the life events you have experienced in the last year and totaling those figures. The higher your score, the more likely you are to experience anxiety, and the more likely your anxiety is to be severe and prolonged. It is important to note that, while the *stressors* are acute in nature, your *responses* to them are not. If your spouse were to die, for example, you could expect to experience some stress for a year after his or her death and, in some cases, even longer.

How severe and prolonged your response to an acute stressor will be depends on many factors. You are likely to experience chronic stress in response to losing your spouse, for example, if your spouse was your or your family's only source of income and if you have limited or no financial resources. On the other hand, social support reduces the effects of stress. The more support you receive from friends and family members, the less severe your reaction to stress is likely to be.

Under what circumstances is acute stress likely to lead to panic attacks? Acute stress leads to panic when you either (1) perceive the situation to be beyond your ability to resolve it or (2) find yourself under chronic stress as a result of the acute stress. To illustrate the first situation, consider a man whose wife has left him. This man believes, and has always believed, that (1) he is basically undesirable and miraculously found this one woman who would marry him; (2) he could never find another woman who would love him as his wife did and whom he would love as he loved his wife; and (3) he cannot live without the love of a woman. It is easy to see that such a man would perceive his wife's leaving as a loss from which there can be no recovery. Laboring under these beliefs, he may well develop panic attacks.

Table 2.1 Social Readjustment Rating Scale

Instructions: Check, in the first column, those life events that have occurred in the past year. Multiply the number of times the event occurred by the Life Change Units. Then add these to obtain a total score.

Life Events	Number of Times Occurred Within the Past Year	Life Change Units		Total
Death of spouse	____	X	100 =	____
Divorce	____	X	73 =	____
Marital separation	____	X	65 =	____
Jail term	____	X	64 =	____
Death of close family member	____	X	63 =	____
Personal injury or illness	____	X	53 =	____
Marriage	____	X	50 =	____
Fired at work	____	X	47 =	____
Marital reconciliation	____	X	45 =	____
Retirement	____	X	45 =	____
Change in health of family member	____	X	44 =	____
Pregnancy	____	X	40 =	____
Sex difficulties	____	X	39 =	____
Gain of new family member	____	X	39 =	____
Business readjustment	____	X	39 =	____
Change in financial state	____	X	38 =	____
Death of close friend	____	X	37 =	____
Change to different line of work	____	X	36 =	____
Change in number of arguments with spouse	____	X	35 =	____
Mortgage over $10,000	____	X	31 =	____
Foreclosure of mortgage or loan	____	X	30 =	____
Change in responsibilities at work	____	X	29 =	____

Table 2.1 Social Readjustment Rating Scale, Continued

Life Events	Number of Times Occurred Within the Past Year	Life Change Units		Total
Son or daughter leaving home	____	X	29 =	____
Trouble with in-laws	____	X	29 =	____
Outstanding personal achievement	____	X	28 =	____
Wife begins or stops work	____	X	26 =	____
Begin or end school	____	X	26 =	____
Change in living conditions	____	X	25 =	____
Revision of personal habits	____	X	24 =	____
Trouble with boss	____	X	23 =	____
Change in work hours or conditions	____	X	20 =	____
Change in residence	____	X	20 =	____
Change in schools	____	X	20 =	____
Change in recreation	____	X	19 =	____
Change in church activities	____	X	19 =	____
Change in social activities	____	X	18 =	____
Mortgage or loan less than $10,000	____	X	17 =	____
Change in sleeping habits	____	X	16 =	____
Change in number of family get-togethers	____	X	15 =	____
Change in eating habits	____	X	15 =	____
Vacation	____	X	13 =	____
Christmas	____	X	12 =	____
Minor violations of the law	____	X	11 =	____
Total Life Change Units			=	____

SOURCE: Adapted from Holmes and Rahe: The social readjustment rating scale. *Journal of Psychosomatic Research*, 1967, pp. 213–218, 227. Courtesy of Pergamon Press.

To illustrate the second situation, consider a woman who has been fired from her third job in a year. She is now out of work and facing the prospect of finding another job without references. Being unemployed represents chronic stress on the heels of an acute stressor—being fired.

Understanding the role that acute stressors play in the development of your panic attacks is important to your learning how to deal with these attacks. Critical to treatment is your perception that the stressor represents a problem you can solve. If an acute stressor becomes chronic stress because you perceive the problems it creates as unresolvable, treatment must be aimed at improving your ability to solve such problems.

Acute stress can also lead to panic attacks when you have a learned vulnerability to the symptoms themselves. Consider Ron, a man whose father had died of a heart attack. Because of acute stress in his own life, Ron developed panic attacks, with his symptoms including rapid heart rate, chest tightness, and chest pain. Perhaps because of his father's fatal heart attack, Ron immediately assumed that he too was having a heart attack, a belief that increased his overall level of anxiety. In spite of self-reassurances to the contrary, every time Ron began to feel his chest tighten or his heart rate increase, he automatically concluded that he was having a heart attack, causing his anxiety level to jump further and inducing a panic attack.

Chronic Stress and No-Win Conflicts

If you suffer from panic attacks, you are likely to find yourself in an apparently unresolvable conflict, a conflict in which any decision you make will result in trouble. You vacillate repeatedly between deciding first one thing, then its opposite. You may well respond to this type of conflict by deciding not to decide—which simply means that you stay in the conflict, whether it be related to staying at or leaving a job, staying in or leaving a marriage, or staying in or leaving a career.

One of my colleagues at the Anxiety Disorders Clinic at Virginia Tech treated a woman named Susan who became engaged to a man whom she doubted she truly loved. Before she knew it, wedding invitations had been sent out, a wedding dress purchased, all arrangements made, and she was married. Immediately after the distraction of making arrangements was gone, she knew that she had made a mistake. She began to feel trapped, a feeling she responded to by developing panic attacks. Consider her dilemma. On the one hand, she felt tremendous social pressure. She had had a large wedding and had received many gifts. If she terminated her marriage, she would have to face the great embarrassment of returning all the gifts. Also, the marriage was not a day old before she knew it was a mistake. How could she acknowledge publicly that her judgment had been so poor? On the other hand, she was faced with the prospect of living with a man she didn't love for the rest of her life. Interestingly enough, the panic attacks themselves served to distract her from deciding whether or not to end her marriage. The whole process continued for months before she was able, with the help of her therapist, to end the charade. In this and numerous other cases, chronic stress leads to panic attacks when the person feels trapped.

Mary, whom we met earlier, provides another example of how chronic stress can lead to panic attacks. Mary had developed a lifestyle of doing more and more in less and less time. Individuals who create this type of stress for themselves are typically hard-driving professionals and business people, perfectionists in middle-management jobs who have to please an assortment of different people, and people who try to combine two careers while driving themselves to do both perfectly. Individuals in these situations seldom have well-defined personal goals and, as a consequence, never feel satisfied with their accomplishments. They are like the horse with the carrot dangling eternally in front of them, never getting their reward but sure as hell running hard to try.

Hassles represent still another type of chronic stressor. Hassles refer to events—often daily events—that gradually wear down our individual reserves. Hassle upon hassle can trigger a major stress reaction in the form of an extended episode of anxiety or depression. Research has shown that daily hassles can diminish your emotional well-being significantly.

To measure your level of daily hassles, consult Table 2.2. As you can see, the Hassles Scale includes a variety of common daily events. When encountered often, they are hazardous to your health and can precipitate panic attacks.

Idiosyncratic Stress and Learned Vulnerability

Idiosyncratic stress refers to the special vulnerability each of us has to specific kinds of stress. As such, idiosyncratic stress can be either acute or chronic. All stress is in a sense idiosyncratic: after all, you must perceive something as stressful before you experience stress. An event you perceive as stressful another might see as an opportunity, although some consensus does exist on events that most people tend to consider stressful, as illustrated by the Holmes and Rahe scale (Table 2.1).

Your past history is your key to understanding (1) why some stress triggers a feeling of panic in you, and (2) why experiencing panic symptoms leads you to fear future panic episodes—the "fear of fear" response. Your personal history teaches you to experience the panic attack itself as a stressor, and a terrifying one at that.

Table 2.2   The Hassles Scale

Directions: Hassles are irritants that can range from minor annoyances to fairly major pressures, problems, or difficulties. They can occur a few or many times.

   Listed in the center of the following pages are a number of ways in which a person can feel hassled. First, circle the hassles that have happened to you *in the past month.* Then look at the numbers to the right of the items you circled. Indicate by circling a 1, 2, or 3 how severe each of the *circled* hassles has been for you in the past month. If a hassle did not occur in the last month do not circle it.

Hassles	Severity 1. Somewhat severe 2. Moderately severe 3. Extremely severe		
1. Misplacing or losing things	1	2	3
2. Troublesome neighbors	1	2	3
3. Social obligations	1	2	3
4. Inconsiderate smokers	1	2	3
5. Troubling thoughts about your future	1	2	3
6. Thoughts about death	1	2	3
7. Health of a family member	1	2	3
8. Not enough money for clothing	1	2	3
9. Not enough money for housing	1	2	3
10. Concerns about owing money	1	2	3
11. Concerns about getting credit	1	2	3
12. Concerns about money for emergencies	1	2	3
13. Someone owes you money	1	2	3
14. Financial responsibility for someone who doesn't live with you	1	2	3
15. Cutting down on electricity, water, etc.	1	2	3
16. Smoking too much	1	2	3
17. Use of alcohol	1	2	3
18. Personal use of drugs	1	2	3
19. Too many responsibilities	1	2	3
20. Decisions about having children	1	2	3
21. Non–family members living in your house	1	2	3
22. Caring for a pet	1	2	3
23. Planning meals	1	2	3
24. Concerned about the meaning of life	1	2	3
25. Trouble relaxing	1	2	3
26. Trouble making decisions	1	2	3
27. Problems getting along with fellow workers	1	2	3
28. Customers or clients giving you a hard time	1	2	3
29. Home maintenance (inside)	1	2	3
30. Concerns about job security	1	2	3
31. Concerns about retirement	1	2	3

Table 2.2 The Hassles Scale, Continued

Hassles	Severity 1. Somewhat severe 2. Moderately severe 3. Extremely severe		
32. Laid-off or out of work	1	2	3
33. Don't like current work duties	1	2	3
34. Don't like fellow workers	1	2	3
35. Not enough money for basic necessities	1	2	3
36. Not enough money for food	1	2	3
37. Too many interruptions	1	2	3
38. Unexpected company	1	2	3
39. Too much time on hands	1	2	3
40. Having to wait	1	2	3
41. Concerns about accidents	1	2	3
42. Being lonely	1	2	3
43. Not enough money for health care	1	2	3
44. Fear of confrontation	1	2	3
45. Financial security	1	2	3
46. Silly practical mistakes	1	2	3
47. Inability to express yourself	1	2	3
48. Physical illness	1	2	·3
49. Side effects of medication	1	2	3
50. Concerns about medical treatment	1	2	3
51. Physical appearance	1	2	3
52. Fear of rejection	1	2	3
53. Difficulties with getting pregnant	1	2	3
54. Sexual problems that result from physical problems	1	2	3
55. Sexual problems other than those resulting from physical problems	1	2	3
56. Concerns about health in general	1	2	3
57. Not seeing enough people	1	2	3
58. Friends or relatives too far away	1	2	3
59. Preparing meals	1	2	3
60. Wasting time	1	2	3
61. Auto maintenance	1	2	3
62. Filling out forms	1	2	3
63. Neighborhood deterioration	1	2	3
64. Financing children's education	1	2	3
65. Problems with employees	1	2	3
66. Problems on job due to being a woman or man	1	2	3
67. Declining physical abilities	1	2	3
68. Being exploited	1	2	3
69. Concerns about bodily functions	1	2	3

Continued

Table 2.2 The Hassles Scale, Continued

Hassles	Severity 1. Somewhat severe 2. Moderately severe 3. Extremely severe		
70. Rising prices of common goods	1	2	3
71. Not getting enough rest	1	2	3
72. Not getting enough sleep	1	2	3
73. Problems with aging parents	1	2	3
74. Problems with your children	1	2	3
75. Problems with persons younger than yourself	1	?	3
76. Problems with your lover	1	2	3
77. Difficulties seeing or hearing	1	2	3
78. Overloaded with family responsibilities	1	2	3
79. Too many things to do	1	2	3
80. Unchallenging work	1	2	3
81. Concerns about meeting high standards	1	2	3
82. Financial dealings with friends or acquaintances	1	2	3
83. Job dissatisfactions	1	2	3
84. Worries about decisions to change jobs	1	2	3
85. Trouble with reading, writing, or spelling abilities	1	2	3
86. Too many meetings	1	2	3
87. Problems with divorce or separation	1	2	3
88. Trouble with arithmetic skills	1	2	3
89. Gossip	1	2	3
90. Legal problems	1	2	3
91. Concerns about weight	1	2	3
92. Not enough time to do the things you need to do	1	2	3
93. Television	1	2	3
94. Not enough personal energy	1	2	3
95. Concerns about inner conflicts	1	2	3
96. Feeling conflicted over what to do	1	2	3
97. Regrets over past decisions	1	2	3
98. Menstrual problems	1	2	3

Some examples will help illustrate how idiosyncratic stress develops. Jennifer had spontaneous panic attacks as well as a history of feeling panicky in airplanes. Her panicky feeling in airplanes was not born of a fear that the plane would crash but rather that she would become anxious and vomit, a case of fearing fear. A careful examination of her history revealed that as a young girl she flew frequently,

Table 2.2 The Hassles Scale, Continued

Hassles	Severity 1. Somewhat severe 2. Moderately severe 3. Extremely severe		
99. The weather	1	2	3
100. Nightmares	1	2	3
101. Concerns about getting ahead	1	2	3
102. Hassles from boss or supervisor	1	2	3
103. Difficulties with friends	1	2	3
104. Not enough time for family	1	2	3
105. Transportation problems	1	2	3
106. Not enough money for transportation	1	2	3
107. Not enough money for entertainment and recreation	1	2	3
108. Shopping	1	2	3
109. Prejudice and discrimination from others	1	2	3
110. Property, investments or taxes	1	2	3
111. Not enough time for entertainment and recreation	1	2	3
112. Yardwork or outside home maintenance	1	2	3
113. Concerns about news events	1	2	3
114. Noise	1	2	3
115. Crime	1	2	3
116. Traffic	1	2	3
117. Pollution	1	2	3
Have we missed any of your hassles? If so, write them in below:			
118. _____	1	2	3
One more thing: Has there been a change in your life that affected how you answered this scale? If so, tell us what it was:			

SOURCE: Adapted from Kanner, A. D., Coyne, J. C., Schaefer, C., & Lazarus, R. S. (1987). Comparison of two modes of stress management: Daily hassles and uplifts versus major life events. *Journal of Behavioral Medicine*, 24–29. Courtesy of Plenum.

without difficulty, often with her father. She recalled one particular instance of flying with her father after she, her mother, and her sister had moved to another state "for a visit." Though young, Jennifer recalled knowing that her mother had left her father and that this flight with her father would be the last for a long time. She became nauseated on the flight and then began thinking that her father would never again be available to soothe her during a flight. When Jennifer became an adult, her panic and fear of losing control were directly related to panic over the loss of her father. Her spontaneous panic attacks were related to her belief that the needy, dependent behavior she adopted when she feared losing her relationship with a man inevitably drove the man away. She was convinced that she would never have a long-term relationship with a man and repeatedly acted in ways to ensure that her self-fulfilling prophecy would come true.

In a second example, a man named Roger developed panic attacks while driving his car, especially at night or when he was tired. He explained, reasonably enough, that he was afraid of having an accident under those conditions, as he had some difficulty seeing at night. Further questioning revealed, however, that one of his best friends in college had died in an automobile accident driving home after the semester had ended. Roger had pleaded with him not to make the trip that night. Roger feared that he too would die if he drove at night or while he was tired. In both of these examples, the mundane events of driving a car or flying in an airplane became terrifying because they were associated with stressful prior life events.

Your personal history can also reveal why you experience the symptoms themselves of a panic attack as terrifying. Since a great many people probably experience the physiological symptoms of panic without panicking, the question naturally arises as to why some people do panic. The answer seems to lie in each person's *interpretation* of his or her symptoms. Some examples we have already seen will help demonstrate why their somatic symptoms terrify some people.

Ralph, if you remember, had been hospitalized for depression and had experienced the hospitalization itself as terrifying. Ralph mistook his symptoms of panic as evidence that he was "going crazy," would "have to be locked up forever," and would "always be that way." Ron, whose father had died of a heart attack, interpreted his own symptoms of chest pain and tension as evidence that he was also vulnerable to heart disease and that he, too, would die young. Jean, sensitive to the opinions of others, was certain that her symptoms "were obvious to everyone" and would "make people laugh at her and think she was weak." These thematic fears bespeak a learned vulnerability to the symptoms themselves and a readiness to perceive the symptoms as threatening. This conditioned readiness to respond to stressors leads to the "fear of fear."

We have seen that people who suffer from panic attacks learn to respond to certain stressors with panic because they associate those stressors with stressful prior life events. Most people, however, experience similarly stressful life events without developing panic attacks. Why do some people develop panic attacks while others do not? The answer may lie in another realm of learning, that of early childhood, in which we construct our basic belief systems.

In the case of Ralph, his father had coaxed and cajoled him into working when he had not wanted to, and he had complied. Although Ralph complied, his father's attitude toward him did not change; he remained critical and aloof. Ralph's task in life was to please his father regardless of the cost to him and regardless of the unattainability of his father's acceptance. When he married to escape his life at home, Ralph found himself dominated by a woman whose expectations felt to him like royal proclamations—neglected only at his extreme peril. His fear of being rejected guided his life, and when this fear clashed with his own sense of what was good for him, he faced a no-win situation. Without his early experiences, would Ralph's marriage have become the trap that triggered his panic attacks? While possible, it would have been much less likely. What Ralph learned early on from his experiences with his father was to expect dire consequences if he listened to his own messages. He had been conditioned to expect and perceive rejection. Another human being stating a preference was enough to start him imagining the worst scenario possible if he stated an objection.

Ralph's situation is typical of many panic attack sufferers. Early learning as well as later experiences prepare the way for vulnerabilities to develop. When the vulnerable person encounters new stress, panic often results. What kinds of stress typically lead a person to panic, therefore, offer clues to the source of the person's vulnerability. Vulnerabilities that lead to panic typically spring from inaccurate beliefs about how you must and must not behave. We can identify at least four basic inaccurate beliefs.

1. *I can't live without him/her.* If you believe you can't live without someone, you also believe you can't exist on your own, and you are thus vulnerable to loss. What life experiences prepare the way for such a belief? Some possibilities include (a) witnessing a parent become mentally ill after a divorce or the death of a family member, (b) the repeated loss of important people in your life, and (c) being given the constant message that you are inadequate. In this last example, you learn that approval follows only when you agree with your parent, teacher, or supervisor. Agree with an authority figure and you're OK. Disagree with an authority figure and he or she will reject not only your ideas but also you yourself. In this way, you come to believe that you are wrong and, especially, that you are always wrong when you disagree with authority. Furthermore, you gradually come to attribute your being wrong to your own basic inadequacy. Any threatened loss, through death, sickness, divorce, or emotional withdrawal, activates your sense of nonself and your belief in your manifest inadequacy.

How can you deal with the everyday problems of life alone? It's time to panic.

2. *I can't lose control!* You believe that if you lose control in any way people will judge and humiliate you. You will be laughed at, considered crazy or different, or shunned. The training for such a belief system usually begins early. Controlling your emotions is a cardinal rule of your early training. Crying, getting angry, and even laughing are out of the question. If you break this rule, your parents shame and ridicule you. Other people who lose control are labeled ineffectual, rude, disrespectful, social outcasts, or crazy. They may be spoken of in whispers and derided for their inappropriate behavior. As a child growing up in this environment, you need not be the direct recipient of such treatment to learn your lesson. All that is necessary is that you see others treated in this fashion. Conforming behavior—the model child—is often typical of those who hold this belief. When you feel anxiety later on, however minimally, you interpret it as a signal that you are about to lose control, and all your alarms sound. Your first thought is of what other people will think, and, of course, your conclusion is automatic: they will think you laughable or worse.

3. *I must be successful, but I can't be!* This belief is just as often learned from a parent's model as from direct messages. A father or mother who is driven to succeed but never does is the most likely source of this belief. You are simply expected to be a carbon copy of your parents, and you learn to fit in without so much as asking yourself if you want to. Goals are never well defined. Achieving all isn't good enough, but what is good enough is never made clear. When you have grown up with this insidious message, you often can't define the source of your problem. You find yourself discontented and responding to your discontent by constantly increasing your activities until you crash. The payoffs for this behavior (after all, society rewards productivity) make changing it—or even recognizing that such change is desirable—difficult.

4. *I must never disappoint.* If you believe this, you generally have a positive image of yourself. You have been rewarded for taking care of others, and this strategy has worked well for you. You are generous, and you anticipate others' needs, usually before they anticipate yours. You almost never say what you want or don't want. You simply haven't had much practice in doing that. You've been too busy making your way by taking care of others. This role is often chosen consciously or unconsciously by the person who adopts the role. A brother or sister has taken the role of the family black sheep, you've seen its effect on your family, and you've decided to make amends for everything and everyone. You become the arbitrator in the family, the diplomat who tries to make everything run smoothly, who soothes the ruffled feelings of all concerned. Problems only arise when you wake up one day

and realize that no one is taking care of you. You have never learned how to get taken care of. The stress of taking care of everyone else typically leads to a decision to leave your relationship or job. Having learned to take care of and not disappoint others, you feel trapped by the seeming impossibility of having your needs met in your relationship or job, and you come to the conclusion that to meet your needs you will have to leave. Leaving, however, means hurting those you've always taken care of, a prospect that may seem too painful to contemplate. In addition, you may subconsciously suspect that even if you were to leave you would likely put yourself in the same situation all over again. The only way to maintain your sense of self is by being alone, but you have defined your life in relation to being with and taking care of others. The belief that you may not disappoint others thus, again, leaves you in a no-win situation.

Each of the above learned belief systems paves the way for the development of panic attacks. The belief systems alone, however, do not cause panic attacks; only in the presence of some critical stress are they likely to lead to panic. Furthermore, the stress must be of a particular kind, one that fits with the belief system. This is why panic attack sufferers wonder, aloud and to themselves, "Why this stress? I've survived a hundred other situations with no problems. Why am I falling apart now?" Another answer to the question "Why now?" may lie in yet another question: "What is your general psychological adjustment when the critical stress strikes?"

Depression

We have seen that depression frequently seems to precede as well as accompany or follow panic attacks; a wide variety of research studies also confirms this. Why is this so? Let's first see why depression follows panic. Panic attack sufferers report that repeated panic attacks make them feel out of control, causing them to avoid going out and to feel more out of control. When you feel out of control, depression generally follows. In addition, panic attacks raise your overall level of stress and reduce your overall level of emotional well-being. A somewhat different scenario occurs when depression precedes panic attacks.

Depression has two effects when it precedes panic attacks. Being depressed in itself can make you feel out of control, a particular vulnerability of panic attack sufferers. It also increases your vulnerability to stress by lowering your resistance and acting as a stressor itself. When you are depressed, you often cannot sleep or eat, further lowering your resistance to stress. Solving problems is difficult when you have slept an average of only two hours a night for a month or when you have lost 15 pounds in two weeks. In addition, people who have been depressed and who have recovered from it often fear a recurrence of their depression.

This fear can itself trigger a panic attack when your memory of your depression is vivid. One woman, hospitalized for depression, interpreted any period of sadness as a loss of control that heralded another major depressive episode. She responded to periods of sadness with a variety of catastrophic thoughts, including "I'm going crazy. I'll be locked up forever. This time I'll never recover." These thoughts were sufficient to produce panic attacks, which then increased both her sense of being out of control and her depression and led to further attacks.

Summary

What causes panic? The best answer is that a number of factors combine to produce panic attacks. They include:

1. *Genetic predisposition:* Panic attacks do run in families but to a limited degree. Most relatives of people with panic attacks do not have panic attacks.
2. *Chemical factors:* These include excessive caffeine intake, vulnerability to sodium lactate, and alcohol and drug abuse.
3. *Physical problems:* A variety of common physical problems can lower your body's resistance and render you more vulnerable to panic attacks. These may precede the onset of the first attack or increase your chances for further attacks once you have developed a pattern of having panic attacks.
4. *Stress:* Both chronic stress and acute stress with long-term effects have been found to precede the onset of panic attacks.
5. *Learned vulnerabilities:* These pave the way for specific stressors to trigger panic attacks and determine what kinds of stressors will trigger attacks. Learned vulnerabilities usually take the form of inaccurate belief systems.
6. *Depression:* When already weakened by depression or other emotional problems, you are more vulnerable to experiencing panic attacks.

3

The Symptoms of Panic

*T*he most distressing and frightening aspect of a panic attack is the physical aspect, the bodily changes you experience during the course of an attack. We began our examination of these symptoms in Chapter 1. Here we examine them more closely so that you can better understand what the symptoms are, how to measure their severity, and what you may be doing to induce them. Recognizing the symptoms and their dynamics will help make them less frightening. Understanding how they develop, and especially what you do to bring them on, will enable you to adopt strategies to reverse the process and gain control over them.

Measuring Your Symptoms

What are the main symptoms of your panic attacks? Do you mostly have trouble breathing, problems with your heart pounding or racing, or problems with nausea? How severe are your panic attacks? Are they getting better or worse?

To understand your attacks, you must assess whether your symptoms vary from one attack to another or remain the same. To know whether your panic attacks are changing or staying the same, and whether they are getting more severe or improving, you must assess them regularly using a reliable measure. At the Anxiety Disorders Clinic at Virginia Tech, we have been measuring the severity of attacks using the Panic Attack Symptoms Questionnaire (PASQ), shown in Table 3.1.

You can determine the severity of each of your panic attacks by rating each symptom on the questionnaire. Notice that you rate each symptom according to its duration: the longer the symptom lasts the more severe it is. Notice also that this questionnaire contains many more symptoms of panic than were listed in Chapter 1. Panic attack

Table 3.1 The Panic Attack Symptoms Questionnaire

Instructions: The symptoms listed below are frequently experienced during a panic attack. Using the scale below for your most recent attack, circle the number corresponding to the length of time you experienced any of the symptoms listed.

	Do Not Experience This	Fleetingly (1 sec–1 min)	Briefly (1 min–10 min)	Moderately (10 min–1 hr)	Persistently (1 hr–24 hrs)	Protractedly (1 day–2 days or longer)
1. Heart beating rapidly	0	1	2	(3)	4	5
2. Pain in chest	0	1	(2)	3	4	5
3. Heart pounding in chest	0	1	2	3	(4)	5
4. Difficulty in swallowing (lump in throat)	(0)	1	2	3	4	5
5. Feeling of suffocation	(0)	1	2	3	4	5
6. Choking sensation	(0)	1	2	3	4	5
7. Hands or feet tingle	(0)	1	2	3	4	5
8. Face feels hot	(0)	1	2	3	4	5
9. Sweating	(0)	1	2	3	4	5
10. Trembling or shaking inside	0	(1)	2	3	4	5
11. Hands or body trembling or shaking	0	(1)	2	3	4	5
12. Numbness in hands or feet	0	(1)	2	3	4	5
13. Feeling that you are not really you or are disconnected from your body	0	1	2	(3)	4	5
14. Feeling that things around you are unreal, as if in a dream	0	1	(2)	3	4	5
15. Vomiting (not induced)	(0)	1	2	3	4	5
16. Nausea	0	1	2	3	(4)	5
17. Breathing rapidly (as if unable to catch your breath)	0	1	2	3	(4)	5
18. Cold hands or feet	0	1	2	3	(4)	5
19. Dry mouth	0	1	2	3	4	(5)

Table 3.1 The Panic Attack Symptoms Questionnaire, Continued

	Do Not Experience This	*Fleetingly (1 sec–1 min)*	*Briefly (1 min–10 min)*	*Moderately (10 min–1 hr)*	*Persistently (1 hr–24 hrs)*	*Protractedly (1 day–2 days or longer)*
20. Sinking feeling in stomach	0	1	2	3	4	5
21. Nerves feeling "wired"	0	1	2	3	4	5
22. Feeling physically immobilized	0	1	2	3	4	5
23. Blurred or distorted vision	0	1	2	3	4	5
24. Pressure in chest	0	1	2	3	4	5
25. Numbness in body (other than in hands or feet)	0	1	2	3	4	5
26. Shortness of breath	0	1	2	3	4	5
27. Dizziness	0	1	2	3	4	5
28. Feeling faint	0	1	2	3	4	5
29. Butterflies in stomach	0	1	2	3	4	5
30. Stomach knotted	0	1	2	3	4	5
31. Tightness in chest	0	1	2	3	4	5
32. Legs feeling wobbly or rubbery	0	1	2	3	4	5
33. Feeling disoriented or confused	0	1	2	3	4	5
34. Cold clamminess	0	1	2	3	4	5
35. Sensitivity to loud noises	0	1	2	3	4	5
36. Ears ringing	0	1	2	3	4	5

37. Other (please list) _____

How many times have you experienced these attacks:

in the past week _____

in the past month _____

in the past 6 months _____

in the past year _____

sufferers actually report a much larger number of symptoms than is listed in the DSM-III-R.

Here's how to use this scale to measure the severity of any panic attack:

1. Identify your most recent attack.
2. Rate each symptom of this attack according to how long each persisted.
3. Total your scores for all symptoms.

Compare your final score with the following scale:

Mild attack = 69 or below
Moderate attack = 70–108
Severe attack = 109 or above

What is meant by a mild, moderate, or severe attack? A severe attack is one in which you experience a large number of symptoms for a long time; in a mild attack, your symptoms are fewer, of shorter duration, or both. The range of scores that represent a moderate attack was determined by asking a large number of people who have panic attacks to rate the symptoms of their last attack using the PASQ. The average attack for this group was found to range from 70 to 108. More rarely, these panic attack sufferers had milder or more severe attacks.

Classifying Your Symptoms

Though you may experience all of the symptoms listed in the PASQ during a single panic attack, more likely, you will experience only some of them. These symptoms may change over time but will tend to fall into groups or sets of symptoms called symptom clusters. If you have one of the symptoms in a cluster, you are likely to also have the other symptoms in that cluster. Not all of the symptoms in the PASQ fall into one of the clusters, while some symptoms fall into more than one cluster. Knowing what clusters characterize your attacks will help you determine what coping strategies to apply. We will see in Chapter 8 how you can tailor specific coping strategies to specific symptoms.

Below are listed the six symptom clusters that characterize different kinds of panic attacks:

Cluster A: *Disorientation*
   Feeling of suffocation (5)
   Feeling that you are not really you or are disconnected from your body (13)
   Feeling that things around you are unreal, as if in a dream (14)
   Dizziness (27)

Feeling faint (28)
Disorientation or confusion (33)
Ears ringing (36)
Cluster B: *General Autonomic Arousal*
Heart beating rapidly (1)
Heart pounding in chest (3)
Feeling of suffocation (5)
Trembling or shaking (10)
Hands or body trembling or shaking (11)
Breathing rapidly (17)
Shortness of breath (26)
Cold clamminess (34)
Cluster C: *Stomach Distress*
Sinking feeling in stomach (20)
Nerves feeling "wired" (21)
Butterflies in stomach (29)
Stomach knotted (30)
Cluster D: *Numbness or Tingling*
Hands or feet tingling (7)
Numbness in hands or feet (12)
Numbness in body other than in hands or feet (25)
Cold clamminess (34)
Cluster E: *Chest Discomfort*
Pain in chest (2)
Pressure in chest (24)
Shortness of breath (26)
Tightness in chest (31)
Cluster F: *Nausea*
Face feels hot (8)
Nausea (16)
Breathing rapidly (17)

Most people who have panic attacks experience the symptoms in Cluster B, which include changes in heart rate and breathing as well as trembling or shaking. Also common are Cluster A symptoms, associated with disorientation. Mild attacks typically include only one or two clusters. The specific symptom clusters that characterize a given person's attacks tend to remain constant, but as a person's attacks become milder, he or she experiences symptoms from fewer clusters and for shorter periods of time.

An example will illustrate this process. Tim had severe and frequent attacks for two weeks before he entered treatment. His attacks occurred at least once a day and often twice. He described each attack as beginning with a feeling that his chest was being squeezed in a vice: his chest was tight and he had trouble breathing (Cluster E).

Immediately, he would feel his heart pounding hard and fast (Cluster B). He reported feeling strange and weird, as if he were walking and talking in slow motion (Cluster A). He feared he was having a heart attack, as within minutes his hands became numb (Cluster D), his face became hot, (Cluster F) and he began to feel nauseated (Cluster F). His attacks followed this pattern with little variation until he entered treatment. Within a week, his attacks were fewer and milder. After one week, he still reported feeling strange, had difficulty getting a full breath, and experienced tightness in his chest. Gone, however, were his hot flashes, his nausea, and the numbness in his hands.

Let's see how you can apply this kind of assessment to yourself. You have already used the PASQ to measure the symptoms of your last panic attack. Now you can find out what symptom clusters characterize your attacks. To do so, get an average score for each of the symptom groups. For your convenience, each of the items in the list of clusters is followed by a number that corresponds to its number in the PASQ. To see if disorientation was a significant factor in your last panic attack, for example, get a total score for all the symptoms in Cluster A and divide that figure by the number of items in this group. Thus, if you rated each of the symptoms belonging to the disorientation cluster as a 4, you would have an average score of 4, which, as the PASQ indicates, would mean that, during your last attack, each symptom in that cluster lasted an average of 10 minutes to 1 hour. Any cluster with an average score less than 2 was not a significant component of your attack. Clusters with an average score between 2 and 4 represent important components of your attack, and any symptom cluster with an average score greater than 4 was a dominant feature of your attack. As you repeat this process for each of the clusters, you may find that some of the symptom clusters are simply not typical of your attacks. Such information is helpful, because it enables you to concentrate your coping strategies on those symptom clusters that truly are a part of your problem. Figuring out which clusters are significant for you and which are not will give you a clear picture of how you experience panic attacks.

The Problem of Contagion

Contagion refers to a phenomenon in which people who experience one group of panic symptoms, when hearing of another group of symptoms, begin to experience or worry that they will experience this other group of symptoms. Like a contagious disease, symptoms can be "caught" from other people. The reason for this phenomenon is unclear but appears to be related to the extreme suggestibility of people who experience panic attacks and to their hypervigilance in looking for symptoms. When you hear of a group of symptoms that you have not experienced, you may become afraid of having those symptoms and start to monitor your body for signs of them. Through a process similar to the contagion of a yawn, you then begin to experience those symptoms.

Armed with the knowledge of this possibility, you will be better able to deal with the problem of contagion should it develop. One way to deal with it is to examine your response when others are discussing symptoms to see if you are indeed experiencing the same symptoms, remind yourself that such things can happen, and use the coping techniques described in the next chapter. For the time being, just being aware of the danger is enough.

Keeping a Record of Your Attacks

Use the Daily Panic Attack Record shown in Table 3.2 to record the frequency and severity of your attacks. This form, which is shorter than the PASQ, will allow you to efficiently track the frequency and severity of your attacks and determine if your attacks are increasing or decreasing. You will use this information when you begin to systematically apply the strategies recommended in this book. If you faithfully record your attacks prior to, while, and after learning the various coping strategies, you will have a much better idea of how your treatment program is working.

The panic symptoms listed on the Daily Panic Attack Record are the same 13 symptoms listed in the DSM-III-R and in Chapter 1. The form allows you to rate up to three separate panic attacks per day, a week at a time. For each attack, rate the duration of each of the 13 symptoms according to the 5-point scale. Notice that this scale differs slightly from the one used in the PASQ. Then total the points to get the severity of each attack.

At the end of each week, count up how many attacks you have had and record the number on the Weekly Panic Attack Record shown in Figure 3.1. Also record the average severity of your attacks for the week. Compute the average severity by adding the total severity scores of all attacks for the week and dividing that sum by the number of panic attacks you had.

Remember, keeping accurate records of your panic attacks will help you notice any changes. Be persistent in your efforts; you are likely to notice changes within several weeks. Most important, however, is that you know how you are doing. Keeping accurate records will enable you to know.

Table 3.2 Daily Panic Attack Record

Week of _____

Panic Symptoms	Monday Attack # 1 2 3	Tuesday Attack # 1 2 3	Wednesday Attack # 1 2 3	Thursday Attack # 1 2 3	Friday Attack # 1 2 3	Saturday Attack # 1 2 3	Sunday Attack # 1 2 3
1. Shortness of breath/smothering sensation							
2. Dizziness/unsteadiness/faintness							
3. Palpitations/fast heart rate							
4. Trembling or shaking							
5. Sweating							
6. Choking							
7. Nausea/abdominal distress							
8. Feelings of unreality							
9. Numbness/tingling							
10. Hot flashes or chills							
11. Chest pain or discomfort							
12. Fear of dying							
13. Fear of going crazy or losing control							
Total Severity							

Scale (total duration): 1 = 1 sec–1 min; 2 = 1 min–10 min; 3 =10 min–1 hr; 4 = 1 hr–4 hr; 5 = 4 hr–1 day

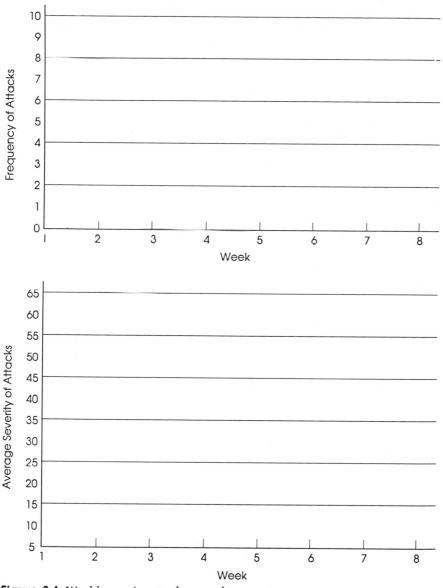

Figure 3.1 Weekly panic attack record

Identifying the Sequence of Your Symptoms

You now have a clearer idea of both the kinds of symptoms that characterize panic in general and the specific symptoms that characterize your own panic attacks. You are now ready to examine the sequence of your symptoms during an attack.

You need to identify the sequence and progression of your symptoms for two separate stages: (1) before a panic attack begins—that is, during the preparatory stage—and (2) from the beginning of a panic attack to the point at which it is most severe. After this point, your symptoms will level off or begin to subside with no significant change in the type of symptoms you are experiencing.

You have seen that a panic symptom can lead to thoughts of an impending attack, which can lead to other symptoms, which in turn lead to catastrophic thoughts. You need to pay attention to this sequence to determine what symptoms you feel first, second, and so on, and what thoughts you have in response to and preceding what symptoms.

As I noted earlier, knowledge is power: knowing your attacks gives you power over them. In identifying the sequence of your symptoms and thoughts, you will learn that your panic attack does, in fact, consist of identifiable parts that follow a distinguishable sequence. With this recognition, you can begin to perceive the attack less as a complete horror and more in terms of various components.

You can begin to trace the sequence of events in your attacks in any of three ways:

1. Put yourself in situations where you have had an attack and wait for one to happen.
2. Induce a panic attack by thinking about the circumstances of your last severe panic attack, including the situation you were in, the symptoms you experienced, and the thoughts you had.
3. Wait for a panic attack to happen.

Using the second of these three alternatives will enable you to make immediate headway in discovering the sequence of your attacks. Some people have trouble reexperiencing their symptoms, so do not be upset if you encounter difficulty. In that case, simply try to remember the string of thoughts, feelings, and events that accompanied a recent attack. Whichever method you use, once you begin to feel anxious, notice which symptom you experience first and which symptoms develop next. Thoughts about what is happening will occur to you immediately. Simply pay attention to them as a passive observer and note what symptoms follow these thoughts. As you pay attention to your symptoms and your thoughts, you will begin to notice that the two are distinct but that one feeds the other. Understanding the particular sequence that your attacks follow will help you to target those symptoms and thoughts that occur early in the sequence and enable you to prevent later symptoms and thoughts from occurring.

To illustrate this process, let's look again at the example of Tim's case. When instructed to recreate his last attack, Tim, using strategy (2), reenacted the following chain of events:

1. He went into a bar with a friend and immediately noticed that the air was full of smoke and the place was crowded and loud.
2. Upon entering the bar, he reexperienced feeling tightness in his chest and difficulty getting a full breath. This time the feeling made sense to him because he related it to the smoke and closeness of the people around him.
3. He thought of getting out—running away—but he felt trapped because his friend wanted to stay.
4. He felt light-headed and flushed. His heart began beating harder and his chest felt tighter.
5. He began wondering if he might have a heart attack.

In recreating this sequence of events, Tim was able to see more clearly the progression of his symptoms and the interplay between the situation, his symptoms, and his thoughts. Though his initial memory clumped all of these together, his recreation allowed him to see that they proceeded in an understandable sequence.

Analyzing Your Preattack Behavior

You will recall that panic attacks are preceded by a preparatory stage of increased conflict and stress. These events set the stage for panic attacks to develop. As you begin to experience panic attacks, your levels of anxiety, tension, and depression are typically elevated. When you find yourself in circumstances in which you have had panic attacks, or in the days before you have a panic attack, your overall level of tension and anxiety increases. You may also be flooded with thoughts about current stresses or conflicts in your life. These symptoms, events, and thoughts are information you can use to help ward off your panic attacks. By becoming aware of the situations, conflicts, thoughts, and feelings that precede a panic attack, you will both better understand why they occur and know when to apply countermeasures.

Analyzing the period immediately before a panic attack is critical, because doing so enables you to learn that *you yourself induce changes in your own body that bring on a panic attack.* Does that seem hard to believe? Time after time, I myself have been amazed, as have my clients, at some of the changes they themselves bring on before an attack. Once you become aware of the changes you induce, altering them is simple. I have identified four common changes: (1) self-induced increases in muscle tension, (2) holding your breath, (3) hyperventilation, and (4) hyperalertness.

Self-Induced Muscle Tension

If, as I have, you talk to a number of people who experience panic attacks while driving, whether it be on highways, over bridges, or in tunnels, you quickly conclude that these people do things to themselves that bring on the attacks. They are almost never aware of what they're doing. You may do similar things when you enter any situation in which you expect to have a panic attack. If you do expect panic attacks in specific situations, analyze those situations. Using some of the techniques we have already discussed (such as, in the case of driving, actually driving on the highway or imagining a familiar drive) you can easily discover what you are doing.

Let's stay with our example of driving to examine this process. Imagine yourself driving in circumstances in which you are likely to have a panic attack (or actually put yourself in these circumstances). Pay attention to your body. What are you doing to yourself? You are preparing for doom. How? By making your muscles as rigid as possible. Observe yourself:

- Do you clutch the steering wheel so hard you cut off circulation to your hands?
- Do you bite holes in your lips or cheeks?
- Do you hunch over the steering wheel with your shoulders, chin, and back locked into position?
- Do your brows furrow and your lips curl into a scowl?

Any of these or other habits that you may add to the list can precede panic attacks, whether while driving or in other situations. They all signal marked increases in muscle tension. Sometimes, such muscle tension persists for days, finally culminating in an attack; at other times, such tension persists for a while, but you do not have a panic attack until you are recovering from the tension. Make no mistake about it. Prolonged muscle tension contributes to your panic attack whether the attack occurs while the tension is still present or after you finally make time to relax.

Tightening your chest muscles can interfere with your ability to breathe. Conduct a simple experiment. First, tighten your chest muscles by flexing your upper chest and shoulders. Next, try to touch your shoulders together in front of you. Now try to take a breath. It is difficult, if not impossible, to get air into your lungs when your chest and shoulder muscles are tightened in this way; yet, people who have panic attacks while driving frequently put themselves in this position. And how do they describe the symptoms they experience during such an attack? They say they can't breathe! The increase in muscle tension they induced before their breathing became difficult is lost to memory.

When, while driving, are you most likely to tense up?

- when you are approaching situations you fear (for example, bridges, tunnels, and stoplights);
- when you are driving fast;
- when you are driving in heavy traffic;
- When you are driving at dusk or at night; or
- when you are driving in unfamiliar surroundings.

The importance of increased muscular tension as a prelude to panic has been demonstrated in people who awake from sleep with panic attacks. A study has shown that such people tense up markedly, as evidenced by the frequency of muscle jerks and twitches, before their panic begins. This study demonstrates that you don't have to be aware of your muscle tension for it to lead to a panic attack.

Once you identify how and when you tense your muscles, you can start taking steps to stop.

1. Loosen your grip on the steering wheel.
2. Relax your mouth and jaw.
3. Remove your teeth from your lip.

Well, you get the idea!

Holding Your Breath

A simple action that often precedes panic attacks, especially panic attacks characterized by breathing difficulties, is holding your breath. Why would you want to hold your breath? Doing so is not a conscious action but an unconscious, automatic response to tension-producing situations. Of course, you can't hold your breath for long periods of time, but you can hold it for short periods—say, 20 to 30 seconds— and take only minute breaths in between.

This creates the sensation that you can't breathe, or, more accurately, that you "can't get a full breath of air." Because your muscles and brain are not receiving enough oxygen, you might also feel light-headed, dizzy, and tense all over. In addition, holding your breath causes the pH level of your blood to change, which can produce a host of symptoms identified with panic attacks.

In any given situation, holding your breath is easier to correct when you have just begun. Once you have been holding your breath for an extended period, getting a full breath can be difficult, indeed.

Hyperventilation

Another way to produce panic symptoms is to hyperventilate. Though hyperventilating can induce a panic attack, it is not dangerous and will not cause physical harm.

What is hyperventilation? Essentially, it is overbreathing, or taking in more oxygen than your body can use. When you hyperventilate, you exhale large amounts of carbon dioxide, thus producing a carbon dioxide deficit in your blood and muscles. It is this deficit that triggers symptoms of panic. A number of people who have panic attacks have been found to (1) hyperventilate as a habit or as a consequence of other physical problems, (2) hyperventilate when they are in stressful situations, or (3) respond to hyperventilation with symptoms of panic.

You can hyperventilate by breathing too rapidly, even if you are taking in only a small amount of air. You can also do so by taking deeper breaths at your normal rate of breathing. Breathing through your mouth is a common cause of hyperventilation, as you can take in more air through your mouth than through your nose. Since breathing through the mouth is a natural consequence of nasal congestion, as can occur with allergies, sinusitis, or other chronic problems, hyperventilation and the symptoms of panic that follow it may increase when those physical problems are acute. Breathing rapidly is normal during physical exertion, because your body's muscles are using the oxygen being taken in. It is also normal in response to emotional arousal, such as when you are in a threatening situation or when you think you are having a panic attack. If you perceive yourself to be in danger, you breathe rapidly as a prelude to either combating the danger or fleeing from it—the well-known fight or flight response.

What symptoms does overbreathing cause? In fact, it affects almost every organ in your body. A partial list of symptoms caused by hyperventilation follows.

1. *General:* fatigue, weakness, exhaustion;
2. *Cardiovascular:* palpitations, rapid heart rate, coldness in one's extremities;
3. *Neurological:* dizziness, light-headedness, numbness and tingling in one's extremities;
4. *Respiratory:* shortness of breath, chest pain, dryness of mouth, yawning, sighing;
5. *Gastrointestinal:* inability to swallow, epigastric pain;
6. *Musculoskeletal:* muscle pains and cramps, tremors, stiffness; and
7. *Psychological:* tension, anxiety, insomnia, nightmares.

As you can see, the symptoms produced by hyperventilation are essentially the same as those that occur during a panic attack. The reduction in carbon dioxide that occurs when you overbreathe causes an increase in the excitability of your nerve cells, which you experience as tingling or numbness in your fingers and toes and around your mouth. Your heart then begins to race, and sounds and colors seem louder and more vivid. These effects are highly unpleasant; sufferers describe them as setting their nerves on edge. As the blood vessels in your brain constrict, you feel light-headed, dizzy, and faint. You may have trouble concentrating. The narrowing of your arteries also means that oxygen is not being carried to your muscles. The muscles of your chest, neck, and arms are likely to feel tense as a result of the reduced oxygen. When these upper body muscles tighten up, your chest feels as if it is in a vice, and you have trouble getting a full breath.

Your first response to such symptoms is, of course, to breathe deeper or faster to get more air into your lungs. This is the worst thing you can do, because it simply aggravates the problem: by breathing more, you only lose more carbon dioxide.

People who chronically hyperventilate are often on the edge of having a panic attack, because the level of carbon dioxide in their blood is always below normal limits. They may be under constant stress from external pressures or from within, have a physical problem, or simply have a bad habit of mildly hyperventilating. For such people, additional, seemingly minor stress may be enough to trigger a panic attack. Because the stress appears insignificant, they experience their panic attack as coming out of the blue.

How can you know if your panic attacks are caused by hyperventilation? Observe your breathing patterns, asking yourself the following questions:

1. Do you breathe through your mouth?
2. While at rest, do you breathe from the upper part of your chest instead of from the lower part?
3. Do you have trouble breathing through your nose?
4. Do you breathe rapidly (18 times or more per minute) while at rest?
5. Do you sigh or yawn frequently?

If you answer yes to any of these questions, you are probably hyperventilating.

Conduct the following experiment: Breathe rapidly through your mouth at least once per second. Continue for one to three minutes. If you experience symptoms similar to those of panic in a minute or less, then at least some of your panic attacks are probably brought on by hyperventilation.

Some people are so susceptible to this last test that they will experience some of the symptoms of panic within seconds after they start. Because of the unpleasantness of the experience, you will be tempted to try it once and then quit. Repeatedly trying to induce panic symptoms in this fashion, however, will result in longer and longer periods before they in fact appear. This occurs for several reasons: (1) you are desensitizing yourself to the experience; (2) in starting and stopping the experience, you are learning that you are in control; and (3) you are introducing coping responses into the cycle, which may include deep breathing or relaxation techniques. As you repeat this test then, you are slowly increasing your ability to start and stop the panic symptoms. We will discuss specific ways of coping with hyperventilation in Chapter 5.

Hyperalertness

Alertness increases with your perception of threat. If you think you are in danger, you automatically begin scouring your environment for signs of that threat. As you do so, your body responds by tensing up and increasing your heart rate and respiration. You have already seen how these events can pave the way for a panic attack.

Hyperalertness both causes and results from the perception of danger. At certain levels, alertness feels good. You are on top of things, in control. As your alertness continues to increase, however, you enter a danger zone.

Driving again provides a good example. Let's say you feel comfortable driving at 45 miles per hour. Because you're late or simply in a hurry, however, you drive at 55. To compensate for your higher speed, you become more alert. If you stay at this speed for a long time, your alertness will trigger other symptoms, like tension in your chest, a headache, or stomach distress. Even if you are aware of these symptoms, you probably aren't aware that they are caused by your alertness. Now imagine that you're still afraid of being late, so you push the accelerator until you hit 65. To compensate, you again increase your attentiveness. You're now hyperalert and perceive every car and truck on the road as a potential threat. Should any slightly threatening incident occur—a car cutting too close to yours, for example— you could find yourself having a panic attack.

As I've said, hyperalertness occurs in response to your perception of threat. If you've had panic attacks, the symptoms themselves can constitute a threat, increasing your alertness to the possibility of having a panic attack. You then become hyperalert to your own body.

This hyperalertness leads to hypochondriasis, a belief that you have something wrong with you even when the sum of evidence indicates that you are well. In this state, you examine every symptom and perceive each as threatening, even commonly experienced symptoms. In this state, all symptoms are evidence of a major physical or mental disorder. One client who scoured his body twice daily for signs of cancer was inspecting his tongue. Sticking it out as far as he could, he noticed numerous bumps on the back of his tongue. Immediately certain that he had cancer of the tongue, he made an appointment with his doctor for a biopsy. Fortunately, his doctor was able to reassure him that the bumps he thought were cancerous were his taste buds.

Not always as ridiculous, hyperalertness, when focused on your body, leads to a chronic increase in tension and an increase in panic attacks. If you look for something hard enough, you're sure to find it—even when it's not there!

Summary

Let's review what you now know about the physical symptoms of panic.

1. The severity of your attacks is measurable. Knowing whether they are getting better or worse will help you evaluate your efforts at getting better.
2. The severity of an attack is primarily a function of two things: the number of symptoms you have and the length of time they last.
3. Panic symptoms tend to occur in clusters, several of which can be identified. These include symptom clusters related to disorientation or feelings of unreality, chest discomfort, stomach distress, nausea, numbness or tingling, and general autonomic arousal.
4. You can determine the sequence that your particular symptoms follow by carefully observing yourself. To make this assessment, you can wait for a panic attack to happen, or you can try to induce some of your symptoms of panic.
5. Once you know what your particular symptoms are and in what sequence they develop, you will feel more in control of your attacks.
6. You may help cause your own panic attacks by unconsciously causing changes in your body. Examples of actions that can lead to panic include self-induced increases in muscle tension, holding your breath, hyperventilation, and hyperalertness.

4

Evaluating Coping Strategies

A number of strategies exist to help you cope with your panic symptoms. The more strategies you have at your disposal, the better able you will be to control your symptoms. In this chapter, we'll first examine what coping strategies are. We'll then develop some rules for determining whether a coping strategy is good or bad. In later chapters, we'll examine some specific characteristics of panic symptoms and panic cognitions. We'll then explore specific coping strategies to help you understand which ones you currently use, which ones you should practice, and which ones you should eliminate from your repertoire.

What Are Coping Strategies?

Essentially, whatever you do to deal with panic is a coping strategy. Taking drugs is a coping strategy! Trying to relax is a coping strategy! Reading the newspaper is a coping strategy!

The tactics of one of my clients—a woman I'll call Adele—illustrate the function of coping strategies.

Adele had severe panic attacks that would sometimes continue for days. Whenever they began, Adele would start doing household chores, trying to distract herself from her symptoms. If doing chores failed to stop her panic attack, Adele would progress to taking long, scalding-hot showers. If this strategy failed, she would exercise, going for a long run or doing aerobics. Exhausted, she would usually find that her attack had subsided sufficiently to allow her to resume her regular activities. If, as sometimes happened, she continued to have a panic attack, she had one last strategy: she inflicted pain on herself in some way—one way was to burn herself with a cigarette. Hurting herself always terminated her attacks.

An unusual story? Absolutely, but it illustrates both the inventiveness of panic attack sufferers and the extremes to which they will go to escape their anxiety. It further illustrates that coping strategies can involve a number of different approaches, that they can be graded in terms of both their effectiveness and their cost to the person using them, and that they can be applied in sequence according to both their effectiveness and cost.

Some people think that a coping strategy is something you do to make things better. Others think that you have to learn coping strategies from an expert before they qualify as coping strategies.

The truth is that *whatever you do to deal with panic is a coping strategy.* Do you

- go to bed?
- leave the situation you are in?
- drink a six-pack?

These are coping strategies! Do you

- start cleaning house?
- turn on the television?
- curl up with a book?

These are coping strategies! Do you

- practice Zen meditation?
- imagine pleasant scenes?
- sit and try to reason out why you're feeling panicky?

These are coping strategies!

If you start to think about it, you will realize that you already have in place a number of techniques for coping with panic attacks. They may not have seemed like coping strategies because no expert told you they were. Or perhaps they have not proven particularly effective, so it didn't occur to you that they might be more effective if systematically applied.

What's So Great About Coping?

In one sense, the term *coping* implies a less-than-satisfactory way of dealing with stress: "How is he doing after his wife's death?" "He's coping!" The implication is clearly that he's just getting by—dealing with the event but minimally. This is not what I mean by coping.

The coping I mean is a way of reducing stress and its consequence—distress. Coping strategies can be effective ways of dealing with both, or they can be ineffective. Optimal coping strategies have two features: (1) they work, and (2) what works is under your control.

If everything you do to deal with panic is a coping strategy, how can you know which strategies to keep, which to discard, which to develop, and which to avoid? Let's see.

Bad Coping Strategies

Clearly, Adele's final coping strategy—hurting herself—is a bad strategy. But what makes it a bad strategy, or any strategy bad? Let's examine some guidelines for determining which strategies to keep and improve and which ones to abandon.

Bad strategies don't work. Bad coping strategies don't succeed in reducing panic symptoms, or they succeed so negligibly that their effect is either fleeting or erratic. They are in effect unreliable.

By this criterion, Adele's final strategy is a good one: it effectively and reliably stopped her panic attacks. But in doing so, it also caused Adele pain and humiliation. Were Adele's other strategies effective? Yes! The fact is that her other strategies also worked, and often. Because they did not work consistently, however, if they did not work right away, she would abandon them.

But how do you know when a coping strategy isn't working? To determine whether or not a coping strategy is working, apply the following steps:

1. Carefully assess the symptoms you are feeling.
2. Assess whether or not you are able to apply the coping strategy.
3. Apply the coping strategy.
4. Give the coping strategy time to work. This usually requires no more than several minutes.
5. Carefully reassess the symptoms you are feeling. If you notice a decline in your symptoms, the coping strategy is working.
6. Continue to apply the coping strategy and monitor its effects.

Bad coping strategies often do not have their intended effect. Since you have probably borrowed many of the coping strategies you use from other situations, some are likely to have no effect on panic attacks.

Let's take an example. One of my clients solved crossword puzzles as a way to relax. After a hard day's work, he found that working crossword puzzles allowed him to unwind. Long after this activity had become habitual, he developed panic attacks. Trying to relax, he naturally turned to crossword puzzles and, in fact, reported that they helped to reduce his panic attacks. Doubting the accuracy of his assessment, I asked him to monitor what happened to his physical symptoms when he worked crossword puzzles during one of his attacks. To his surprise, he found that his symptoms did not change while he was working them and that they actually increased afterward. What had happened to make him think that solving crossword puzzles helped his panic attacks? Apparently, his thoughts distracted him from his symptoms while he worked the puzzles, but when he stopped, they returned. Further, the tension he engendered in solving the puzzles served to increase his panic symptoms once he stopped doing them. Clearly, he was using a coping strategy that didn't work.

Coping strategies assume a clear hierarchy, one that each panic sufferer develops individually. Adele would never inflict pain on herself to stop an attack that had just begun; rather, it was her strategy of last resort. This leads us to a second criterion for determining whether or not a strategy is bad: *bad coping strategies are costly.*

People tend to use some strategies relatively early in the panic sequence. Though ineffective for severe symptoms, with mild symptoms, these strategies work. Other strategies work to reduce panic but people tend to use them only after exhausting other possibilities or in emergencies. But why not use highly effective strategies early in the sequence? The principal reason is that their cost is too high.

What are some high-cost strategies?

- taking drugs or alcohol
- injuring yourself
- eating
- getting emergency treatment

Most of you will have no trouble recognizing the high cost of the examples listed above. Others might, so let me clarify the costs involved. Such strategies are costly for three reasons.

1. These strategies are likely to become habitual and, when habitual, to be directly injurious to body and mind. Habitual consumption of drugs, alcohol, and food are all negative, costly strategies. Each causes major stress on both the body and mind.

Drugs and alcohol pose particular risks because of the way in which people use them as coping strategies. Few people who use drugs and alcohol use them during an attack; rather, they use them in anticipation of an attack. Employed in this way, they are much more likely to become habitual and injure your health.

Why should coping strategies that are used in anticipation of an attack become habitual? The explanation lies in the apparent, but false, success of anticipatory strategies.

Imagine as an example a musician who has had a single isolated panic attack during a performance. Even though she was able to complete her performance successfully, she imagines with horror having another attack at her next performance. She decides to take a drink before each performance to steady her nerves and thus prevent a panic attack. Regardless of how often she has panic attacks while performing, she is likely to conclude that her drinking is helping, in part because alcohol dulls higher brain functions first, making the person feel uninhibited. Further, even if she were to have more frequent attacks, she would likely conclude that an increase in her medicinal dose of alcohol was called for. In this way, coping strategies used in anticipation of an attack are like superstitious acts: the person's perception that they succeed leads him or her to continue them, even though their actual value may be nil.

2. These strategies reduce your sense of self-esteem. High-cost strategies may work, but often the person using them recognizes that they are ultimately destructive. He or she may also view them as a cop out—an easy way to deal with anxiety when a more difficult, but ultimately more satisfying, method could be employed.

One strategy that we have not yet mentioned but that is often despised by its users as a crutch is taking medications to eliminate panic attacks. This is especially true for individuals who fear that if and when they stop taking medication their panic attacks will return. Rather than face this possibility, they continue to take the medication long past the period recommended by their physician and in spite of any side effects they may be experiencing. Using medications in this fashion is a coping strategy that undermines the user's ability to develop internal strategies.

It is, in fact, relying on external coping methods that reduces a person's self-esteem. The person's inability to deal with the stress of these attacks without help paradoxically leads to an increased risk of further attacks. This circular sequence is shown in Figure 4.1. The loss of your belief in your own ability to cope with the attacks reduces your self-esteem and thus increases your vulnerability to future attacks.

3. These strategies prevent you from developing other, more effective strategies. Because almost all strategies are somewhat effective, and some may even be very effective over the short term, people tend to use the same strategies over and over again. People therefore tend to repeat strategies that they discovered early in the development of their panic disorder, often to the exclusion of trying new strategies. In addition to actually reducing anxiety, some techniques offer the individual other payoffs. A man who hates his job, for example, and who has panic attacks at work, may begin taking sick days to stop his panic attacks. His avoiding work successfully eliminates his attacks, at least those that occur at work, and also keeps him away from a job he hates. The chances that such an individual will seek out alternative strategies are small indeed.

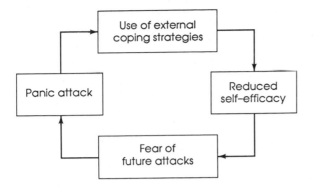

Figure 4.1 External coping strategies and the
panic cycle

Good Coping Strategies

What are good coping strategies? Simply put, they are strategies that
work to reduce your panic attacks. But they have other features as
well. Let's examine what makes a coping strategy a good one.

Good strategies work. Coping strategies that work affect panic attacks in one of two ways. Either they act to prevent attacks, or they
reduce the severity or duration of a panic attack once it has started.
Good coping strategies can also work by reducing both the degree to
which the person anticipates a panic attack and the worry that goes
with such anticipation.

Good strategies work by reducing panic symptoms, panicky
thoughts or both. It is possible to reduce panicky thoughts while leaving panic symptoms unaffected and vice versa. You must, therefore,
be alert to what you are reducing or eliminating with the coping
strategies you are using.

Good strategies leave you feeling in charge. If you feel less in control or more dependent after putting a coping strategy into action,
it is a bad strategy. If you feel more in control of yourself, it is a good
strategy.

There is a term for the belief that you can put into action strategies
that will work to reduce your anxiety: *self-efficacy*. When you believe
that you have the skills to put a coping strategy to work for you, you
have a strong sense of self-efficacy.

Self-efficacy does not require that your strategy succeed, only that
you believe that you can use the strategy appropriately. Notice that
once you buttress your coping repertoire with self-efficacious beliefs,
you are more likely to use the strategies within that repertoire. Further,

you are more likely to feel in charge of yourself, not because you can eliminate any trace of anxiety you might feel, but, rather, because you have skills that you can put into action whenever you do feel anxiety.

When you successfully shift your attention away from the hoped-for end—a reduction in your anxiety symptoms—and toward the process of putting your coping strategies into action, you will have taken a major step toward reducing the severity and frequency of your panic attacks. This is so because shifting your focus from the end point you desire to the action you can take reduces the pressure you feel to succeed. In addition, it places the emphasis where it ought to be—on your own individual effort.

Good strategies work, but they work by having the locus of the change remain in the realm of your own efforts. Taking medication also works, but the locus of the change is in the pill, not in yourself. The same is true of taking a drink before you enter a difficult situation. You are not in charge of dealing with the stress, alcohol is.

Good strategies work in both the short run and the long run. It is easy to see how strategies that function to reduce anxiety work in the short run: they reduce your anxiety. Distraction is one such technique. But what is the long-term effect of relying on a coping strategy like distraction? The message you send yourself is that you are unable to tackle your anxiety directly. Though distraction works, and can, when used consciously, leave you feeling more in charge, it can also have the long-term effect of undermining your belief that you can confront your panic attacks directly.

Let's see how distraction can be a good short-term but bad long-term strategy. Such was the case with Jennifer. Jennifer used distraction to deal with her panicky thoughts as well as her panic symptoms. Whenever she began thinking that she might have a panic attack, she would distract herself from this thought by working. This strategy was helpful over the short term, because as long as she was distracted, she didn't worry about having an attack. She continued to believe, however, that if she allowed herself to think about an attack she would have one. She therefore had to apply her distraction techniques diligently and in the process did not learn that thinking about attacks brings them on. Distraction was in this case the same as avoidance. Rather than increasing Jennifer's sense of self-efficacy, it decreased it.

This, however, is not always the case. Sometimes distraction can be an effective long-term strategy. Such was the case with Mike, who had panic attacks as a consequence of being in a highly stressful job. The job was such that if he wanted to keep it, there was no way of reducing its stressful effects. Mike quickly learned that panic attacks were nothing to be frightened of; he gained control of his thoughts very early on in the process. Nevertheless, he continued to experience periods in which his heart rate, body tension, and feelings of unreality increased for periods of up to an hour. After much trial and error, Mike discovered that distraction in the form of attending to events going on around him was the most effective way of reducing his symptoms. He continued to use this strategy during periods of high work stress that were intermittently punctuated by these episodes of acute panic symptoms. He had confidence in his technique and was therefore able to eliminate any anticipatory anxiety. Distraction in this case proved to be an effective means of dealing with panic over the long term as well as the short term.

The principal difference between a strategy that works over both the long term and the short term and one that works only over the short term is self-efficacy.

Self-Efficacy: The Key to Effective Coping

To cope effectively with your panic attacks, you need to believe that you can put your coping strategies into action. As stated earlier, such a belief is called self-efficacy. The greater your self-efficacy, the more energy you will expend and the longer you will persist in attempting to deal with your panic.

Your self-efficacy varies according to how threatening you perceive your situation to be. If you believe that you can effectively cope with the most severe panic attack you can imagine, your self-efficacy can be said to be very high. If you believe that you can cope with a mild attack but not a severe one, your self-efficacy is proportionately lower. You can gauge your level of self-efficacy for dealing with panic by completing the questionnaire in Table 4-1.

The 11 situations presented in this questionnaire have been graded so that a person requires less self-efficacy to cope with the first items than to cope with the later items. The level of confidence that you indicate in your ability to cope with each situation determines your score. Simply add the numbers you have circled for each of the 11 situations.

This scale is a useful tool for determining how much confidence you have in your ability to cope with panic. Your score should thus rise as you proceed through the exercises in this book. If, at the end of treatment, your self-efficacy score is above 53, you will be in the range of a group successfully treated in our clinic for panic disorder. Prior to treatment, the average self-efficacy score for this group was 29. At the end of treatment, the group's average self-efficacy score was 75, with the scores of those individuals who were successfully treated ranging from 53 to 97.

What sorts of factors affect a person's self-efficacy? There are four, including (1) performance, (2) vicarious learning experiences, (3) verbal persuasion, and (4) emotional arousal.

The most important factor, by far, is the first: performance. Because you experience your own performance directly and receive immediate feedback on how you are doing, this is the main determinant of self-efficacy. For this reason, I have carefully built into my treatment program a gradually more demanding set of challenges related to dealing with panic. Successful completion of each new challenge will increase your self-efficacy.

The other three factors also influence self-efficacy. Observing another individual with panic disorder successfully cope with a diffi-

Table 4.1 Self-Efficacy Questionnaire

Instructions: Think of how you feel right at this moment. Please indicate which of the following parts of a panic attack you believe you could cope with by employing the coping strategies you currently use. Do this by circling either yes or no for each question. Then, after each question, rate how *confident* you are that you could cope by circling one number from 1 to 9.

1. Being in a situation where you've had an attack   yes   no

1	2	3	4	5	6	7	8	9
not at all confident				moderately confident				totally confident

2. First noticing the symptoms of an attack   yes   no

1	2	3	4	5	6	7	8	9
not at all confident				moderately confident				totally confident

3. Having thoughts come into your mind as you experience symptoms, such as thinking you are having a heart attack, dying, and so forth

                                                            yes   no

1	2	3	4	5	6	7	8	9
not at all confident				moderately confident				totally confident

4. Experiencing intense symptoms that continue to worsen and intensify

                                                            yes   no

1	2	3	4	5	6	7	8	9
not at all confident				moderately confident				totally confident

5. Having scary and intense thoughts that continue to occupy your mind

                                                            yes   no

1	2	3	4	5	6	7	8	9
not at all confident				moderately confident				totally confident

cult situation reinforces your belief that you can do so too. Because the treatment program presented here is a self-treatment program, however, vicarious learning (factor 2) has not been incorporated into it. Factors (3) and (4) have, however. Verbal persuasion is, in fact, clearly one of the purposes of writing this book. I want to convince you that you can overcome your panic attacks! Factor (4)—emotional arousal— is based on the observation that a person's performance, and therefore his or her self-efficacy, deteriorates when he or she is aroused or under stress, conditions synonymous with panic attacks. To compensate for this fact, you will be given practice in performing under pressure. Only in this way will you learn to put the emotional arousal that charac- terizes panic attacks to work for you rather than against you.

Table 4.1 (continued)

6. Experiencing symptoms as strong as you have ever felt

yes   no

1	2	3	4	5	6	7	8	9
not at all confident				moderately confident				totally confident

7. Having thoughts as intense, scary, and real as you have ever had

yes   no

1	2	3	4	5	6	7	8	9
not at all confident				moderately confident				totally confident

8. Having a full-fledged attack that lasts 15 minutes   yes   no

1	2	3	4	5	6	7	8	9
not at all confident				moderately confident				totally confident

9. Having a full-fledged attack that lasts 30 minutes   yes   no

1	2	3	4	5	6	7	8	9
not at all confident				moderately confident				totally confident

10. Having a full-fledged attack that lasts several hours

yes   no

1	2	3	4	5	6	7	8	9
not at all confident				moderately confident				totally confident

11. Having a full-fledged attack that lasts all day and seems as though it will not subside   yes   no

1	2	3	4	5	6	7	8	9
not at all confident				moderately confident				totally confident

Summary

Let's review what you have learned about coping strategies in this chapter:

1. Whatever you do to deal with your panic attacks constitutes a coping strategy.
2. Bad coping strategies do not work to reduce panic. People often try to cope with their panic using strategies that have worked for them in other situations but that do not work to reduce their panic.
3. Bad coping strategies are also costly, and their cost outweighs their effectiveness. We examined three ways in which they are costly: (a) they become habitual and, when habitual, are injurious; (b) they reduce your self-esteem; and (c) they prevent you from learning new, more effective strategies.
4. Good coping strategies either prevent attacks or reduce their severity by reducing both your panic symptoms and your panicky thoughts.
5. Good coping strategies also leave you feeling in charge, capable of responding to your panic appropriately. This confidence in your ability to act effectively is called self-efficacy and is essential to your success in coping with panic.
6. Good coping strategies work not only in the short run but also in the long run.
7. Four factors can enhance your self-efficacy in relation to coping with panic: successful performance, vicarious learning experiences, verbal persuasion, and learning to cope with emotional arousal.

5

Coping with the Symptoms of Panic

As you learned in the last chapter, you already possess a number of coping strategies for dealing with your panic attacks. As you become more aware of the strategies you already use, you will gain more conscious control of their use and hence improve their effectiveness. Indeed, the simple process of identifying them as coping strategies will improve their effectiveness. Conscious awareness of your strategies will also allow you to apply them systematically to your panic attacks. In this chapter, we will begin by evaluating the strategies you are currently using to cope with your symptoms. I will then describe some specific additional techniques, step by step, that you can use to cope with your panic symptoms.

What Strategies Do You Use?

In interviewing a number of people suffering from panic disorder, I asked them what they do to deal with their panic symptoms. To my surprise, I found that not only do panic sufferers use a large variety of different strategies, but they are also quite adept at specifying what and how effective the strategies are. From their responses and from research done on coping with stress, I devised a scale, shown in Table 5.1, to measure how frequently people use particular coping strategies to deal with panic and how effectively they reduce symptoms. Once I could measure strategies in this way, I could study which strategies were best for coping with what symptoms.

You will notice that the scale measures three items: (1) the frequency with which you use the strategies, (2) the effectiveness of the strategies in reducing your symptoms, and (3) the effectiveness of the strategies in eliminating your thoughts. In this chapter, I will concentrate on coping strategies that can be used to reduce symptoms, leaving strategies that eliminate thoughts to be examined in a later chapter.

Table 5.1 Coping Strategies Questionnaire

Instructions: (Read carefully.) For each of the strategies listed below, first indicate how often you use the strategy when having a panic attack or how likely you would be to use it if you had one. Next, indicate how effective each strategy was in relieving first your anxiety symptoms and then your anxiety-related thoughts. Use the following scales:

Frequency:	Symptom Reduction:	Thought Elimination:
1 = not used	1 = not effective	1 = not effective
2 = rarely used	2 = somewhat effective	2 = somewhat effective
3 = sometimes used	3 = moderately effective	3 = moderately effective
4 = often used	4 = very effective	4 = very effective
5 = always used	5 = totally effective	5 = totally effective

Remember to rate each item using one number from each of the three scales.

	Frequency	Symptom Reduction	Thought Elimination
1. I tell myself it will pass or it is nothing to worry about.	____	____	____
2. I talk to a physician, psychologist, or other professional.	____	____	____
3. I talk to a friend or relative.	____	____	____
4. I use a formal relaxation technique.	____	____	____
5. I exercise	____	____	____
6. I sit or lie down.	____	____	____
7. I work.	____	____	____
8. I try to reason out what is making me anxious.	____	____	____
9. I try to distract myself mentally by thinking of something else (please specify _____).	____	____	____
10. I try to distract myself by engaging in some activity (please specify _____).	____	____	____
11. I take medication prescribed for anxiety (please specify _____).	____	____	____

	Frequency	Symptom Reduction	Thought Elimination
12. I inflict pain on or in some way injure myself.	___	___	___
13. I drink alcoholic beverages or take street drugs.	___	___	___
14. I splash water on my face.	___	___	___
15. I try to control my breathing.	___	___	___
16. I change positions or make a quick movement.	___	___	___
17. I go outside for fresh air.	___	___	___
18. I leave the situation.	___	___	___
19. I engage in sexual activity.	___	___	___
20. I work on a hobby.	___	___	___
21. I work around the house.	___	___	___
22. I watch television.	___	___	___
23. I eat or drink (something non alcoholic).	___	___	___
24. I try to read.	___	___	___
25. I let the symptoms happen rather than struggle with them.	___	___	___
26. I play a game (not exercise).	___	___	___
27. I just let the attack happen.	___	___	___
28. I try to make the symptoms worse.	___	___	___
29. I tell my thoughts, "Stop."	___	___	___
30. I have someone accompany me in anxiety-provoking situations.	___	___	___
31. I avoid situations that provoke anxiety.	___	___	___
32. I take a bath or shower.	___	___	___

Take the time to complete the questionnaire shown in Table 5.1 according to the instructions. In completing this questionnaire, you will learn that you are already using a variety of coping strategies and that some of them are more effective than others. You may notice immediately that some of the strategies you use frequently may not be particularly effective at reducing your symptoms. You may need to improve the way you implement some strategies, improve your timing in implementing them, or abandon them altogether.

After completing the questionnaire, you can then group your responses according to the following list:

Group A: *Formal Psychological Strategies*
Using a relaxation technique (4)
Exercising (5)
Reasoning out what is making you anxious (8)
Trying to control your breathing (15)

Group B: *Cognitive Strategies*
Telling yourself it will pass (1)
Distracting yourself mentally (9)
Telling my thoughts to stop (32)

Group C: *Physical Distraction Strategies*
Working (7)
Distracting yourself mentally (10)
Splashing water on your face (14)
Changing positions or making quick movements (16)
Going outside for fresh air (17)
Engaging in sexual activity (19)
Working on a hobby (20)
Working around the house (21)
Playing a game (26)

Group D: *Passive Distraction Strategies*
Sitting or lying down (6)
Watching television (22)
Reading a book (24)

Group E: *External Support Strategies*
Talking to a professional (2)
Talking to a family member or friend (3)
Taking prescription medication (11)

Group F: *Acceptance Strategies*
Letting the symptoms happen (25)
Letting the attack happen (27)
Trying to make the symptoms worse (28)

Group G: *Body Abuse Strategies*
Inflicting pain on yourself (12)

> Drinking alcohol or taking street drugs (13)
> Eating or drinking something (23)

Group H: *Avoidance Strategies*
> Leaving the situation you are in (18)
> Having someone accompany you in anxiety-provoking situations (30)
> Avoiding anxiety-provoking situations (31)

Determine what type of strategies you most often use by totaling your responses in the Frequency column for each group of items. (For your convenience, each item is followed in parentheses by its number on the questionnaire.) Then divide the totals for each group by the number of items in the group. Research has shown that people who use one of the strategies in a group are likely to use the other strategies in that group as well; the strategies go together. Evidence also shows that people are more likely to use certain strategies than others to alleviate particular symptoms. Thus, some strategies appear "tailored" to particular symptoms, a characteristic I discuss in Chapter 8. Comparing your average frequency score for each of the coping groups will give you a clear idea of what types of strategies you employ most often.

As you can see from the list, Group A strategies represent more-formal psychological techniques designed to induce relaxation or enhance your understanding of panic attacks. The strategies of Group B are primarily cognitive in nature and target the catastrophic thoughts that accompany panic symptoms. Strategies in this group include telling yourself the symptoms will pass, distracting yourself mentally—such as by thinking of something else—and reasoning to yourself that the symptoms are not threatening, only unpleasant, among other things. These strategies will be explored in detail in Chapter 7. Group C strategies function by distracting you from your panic through some physical activity that requires effort, such as doing housework, or working at a hobby. Physical distraction strategies may also involve exposing yourself to sensory stimuli that compete with panic symptoms, by taking a bath or shower, for example. Group D strategies also involve distraction, but using passive rather than active physical distractions. These passive distractions differ from the mental distractions in Group B in that they focus outside the self instead of on internal thoughts or fantasies. Examples include watching television or reading. Group E strategies involve seeking social support by talking to a spouse, lover, friend, relative, or helping professional. Included in this group of strategies is taking prescription medicine. Group F strategies involve passive or active acceptance of your symptoms.

The strategies of Groups G and H, though used by panic attack sufferers, have been shown to have a negative impact on symptoms over
the long run. Group G strategies involve abusing your body in some
way, such as by hitting or burning yourself, taking street drugs or
drinking alcohol, or eating. Group H strategies are primarily escapist,
including, for example, avoiding situations that you associate with
panic, leaving situations when anticipating a panic attack, and leaving situations when having an attack. Also included is the strategy
of entering situations only in the company of a "safe" person, usually a spouse or family member who knows what the problem is.

Thus, of these eight types of coping strategies, the first six—A
through F—are relatively effective, while the last two—G and H   arc
ineffective.

With the exception of the strategies in Groups G and H, the more
coping strategies you have at your disposal, the better able you will
be to deal with your panic symptoms. Identifying and applying your
strategies clearly and distinctly will help you tailor your strategies
to your symptoms and, further, will enable you to move easily to a
different strategy if the one you are using is proving ineffective. Knowing what strategies you have used successfully in the past is also important; improving on strategies you already have at your disposal
is simply easier than developing entirely new strategies. Let us now
take a systematic look at improving some of the coping strategies we
have identified thus far.

Direct Coping Strategies

The six categories of effective coping strategies listed can be further
split into direct (Groups A and B) and indirect (Groups C, D, and E)
strategies. Direct strategies address panic symptoms directly; indirect
strategies work by directing your attention elsewhere. We will examine
ways of refining both types of strategies, beginning with various direct
coping strategies. The first set of direct coping strategies we will
examine is that of informational strategies, which represent a re-
finement of the Group A strategy "reasoning out what is making you
anxious."

Informational Strategies

Accurate information can help you cope with panic. Three kinds of
information are particularly "strategic," used alone or in combination:

1. What is panic?
2. What causes your panic symptoms?
3. What is really going on during one of your panic attacks?

Using an informational strategy simply means knowing the answers to these questions and deliberately calling upon that information as a means of coping with your panic.

The key to transforming information into knowledge is YOU! To use information about panic attacks as a way of effectively coping with panic, you must do two things. First, you must compare your experiences with that which is known about panic. Second, you must become adept at remembering and using this information during the experience of panic itself. As you come to equate your own experience with the panic experience, you will be able to replace erroneous beliefs about your attacks with accurate knowledge. You must begin, however, by recognizing your experiences as panic. If you continue to believe that your experiences mean that you have a heart disorder, even after your physician has told you that your heart is fine, you will be unlikely to convert the information presented here into knowledge of your own problem. Likewise, if you persist in believing that your panic attacks are a sign of imminent insanity, you will be unlikely to integrate this information into your own experience. On the other hand, if you begin by believing that this information applies to you, you will learn that your panic disorder is a condition within your power to change.

We answered the first question—what is panic?—in Chapter 1. You can answer questions you've had about your own experiences by comparing them with those described in this book. Such information can be so powerful that the knowing alone will eliminate panic attacks in some people.

Knowing what a panic attack is when you're not having one is an accomplishment. Remembering that information when you're having a panic attack represents a much greater accomplishment. During a panic attack, you are in a heightened state of arousal, and you are most concerned with doing whatever you can to stop the feeling. New strategies are likely to be forgotten, or forsaken for old ones. You must, therefore, practice reminding yourself, in situations in which you are experiencing anxiety, of the information you possess. The more practice you get at this, the better at it you will become; the information will become knowledge, and knowing will become habitual.

The answer to the second question—what causes *your* panic symptoms?— is much more individual. I explained in Chapter 2 how you can answer this question for yourself. Here, I want only to remind you of some simple but important distinctions. Panic attacks typically arise in the context of chronic stress. Nevertheless, individual attacks often occur in response to specific stressors or to events such as overexertion or excessive caffeine intake. Knowing such information, you can apply it to each individual attack; for example, regarding your last panic attack:

- Were you particularly bothered by an ongoing conflict?
- Were you under a great deal of time pressure?
- Did you drink too much coffee?
- Had your body been feeling tense prior to the panic attack?
- Had you exercised much more than you were used to?

Having at the ready a series of questions to ask yourself during a panic attack will help you to understand the events that are leading to your attacks. Such knowledge will demythologize your attacks. Furthermore, if you can identify a predictable pattern of events leading to your attacks, you can better prepare yourself to handle these events; for example:

- Figure out a way to resolve the conflict, if only for now.
- Plan your week a little better. Include in it some recreation and relaxation.
- Cut down on your coffee intake, or drink decaffeinated coffee.
- Notice when you are getting tense and take a hot bath.
- Increase the amount of time you exercise slowly so that your body can accommodate to the increased effort.

As you can see, information about the events that lead to your attacks is helpful in several ways, and you can get that information with only a little effort.

Answering the third question—what is really going on during one of your panic attacks?—requires that you carefully observe your own panic attack as if you were outside watching the events taking place in your own body. Doing this will yield information about your symptoms and about your thoughts regarding your symptoms.

Imagine a person making the following observations about a panic attack:

- My heart is pounding right out of my body!
- I can't breathe!
- My heart has stopped!
- I am having a stroke!
- My limbs are paralyzed!

None of these observations is accurate! They are all catastrophic interpretations of what is happening.

Now imagine the same person making another set of observations about the same symptoms:

- My heart is pounding so hard that I can see my chest moving.
- I am having trouble getting a full breath.
- My pulse is faint.
- I can feel the blood throbbing in my head.
- The muscles in my hands are stiff.

None of the above observations is pleasant, but they all are accurate. Further, none of these observations is likely to arouse terror.

You can learn to observe accurately rather than catastrophically by carefully distinguishing between symptoms and thoughts. Ask yourself: Is this a symptom I'm feeling or is this a thought about my symptoms? Once you can make that distinction, you will have taken an important step toward defusing your panic attacks. Try separating your thoughts from your bodily feelings as follows:

- I feel my heart beating hard, and I think, "My heart is beating so hard that it seems as if it's coming out of my chest."
- I feel my head hurting so badly that I think, "It could explode."
- I feel my hands going numb, so I think, "My hands feel as if they're not part of my body."
- My chest feels tight and I can't fill my lungs with air, so I think, "I can't get any air."

When you can make this distinction, and deal with your symptoms and thoughts separately, your attacks lose their overwhelming quality.

Relaxation Strategies

Keep this in mind: you may be aggravating your physical sensations during a panic attack. Panic attack victims have been known to hold their breaths, causing their chests to tighten so they feel unable to breathe; to put their tongues on the roofs of their mouths, blocking air from reaching their lungs; and to breathe rapidly, producing a number of symptoms, including numbness in their hands and feet. So ask yourself, "What am I doing right now to make these symptoms worse?"

Whatever you are doing to aggravate your symptoms, chances are that training yourself to relax would help you stop. To assist you in learning to relax, I will describe in detail three formal relaxation techniques, all direct strategies for coping with your panic symptoms: (1) tensing and releasing, (2) imagery-induced relaxation, and (3) diaphragmatic breathing.

Tensing and Releasing

Many people are not even aware when their muscles are tense. Further, for some people, muscle tension is normal, and relaxation abnormal. Tensing and releasing teaches you to differentiate between having your muscles tensed and being relaxed. The object of this technique is to learn to relax all of your muscles rapidly, in response to a predetermined signal or cue. You will better achieve that object if you take the time to master each step before proceeding to the next. There are four basic steps in this process:

1. Learn to relax specific muscle groups.
2. Learn to relax general groups of muscles.
3. Learn to relax your body as a whole, on cue.
4. Learn to relax specific muscles on cue.

Step 1: Relaxing Specific Muscle Groups. You should perform this exercise sitting rather than reclining—you will have a better chance of applying what you learn to a variety of real-life situations if you practice while sitting—so find a quiet place with a comfortable chair. To learn to relax specific muscles, you first tense the muscle and hold the tension for a count of 5. Then let the muscle go, relaxing it as completely as you can. Hold the relaxation for a count of 10. Do this for each muscle as follows:

Feet and Legs

1. Curl your toes toward the floor.
2. Feel the tension in your toes and feet.
3. Let them go; let them relax.
4. Push both of your heels against the floor.
5. Notice the tension in your lower legs, knees, and thighs.
6. Let those muscles go; let them relax.
7. With your toes on the floor, lift your heels as high as they will go.
8. Feel the tension in your calves.
9. Now let them relax.
10. Flex the muscles in your thighs and hold.
11. Notice the tension in those muscles; pay attention to how it feels.
12. Let those muscles relax.

Buttocks and Stomach

1. Flex the muscles of your buttocks and hold.
2. Notice the tension in those muscles.
3. Let them relax; let them go.
4. Now flex your stomach muscles; make them hard.
5. Notice the feeling; pay attention.
6. Now let them relax; enjoy the sensation.
7. Suck the muscles of your stomach in.
8. Notice the kind of tension this produces.
9. Now let those muscles relax completely.

Chest and Back

1. Push your chest muscles out; make them tight.
2. Notice the feeling of tightness.
3. Now let them relax fully, beyond the point where they were before you tensed them.
4. Next, try to touch your shoulders together in front of you.
5. Notice the tightness in your chest; pay attention to the feeling.
6. Now let those muscles go; let them relax totally.

7. Breathe deeply and let the air out slowly.
8. Enjoy the relief and relaxation that accompanies this process.
9. Now arch your lower back by pushing your stomach out.
10. Feel the tension in your back.
11. Return to your normal position and just let those muscles relax.
12. Press your back against the chair.

Shoulders and Neck

1. Shrug your shoulders and hold that position.
2. Feel the tension in your shoulders.
3. Now release them and let them relax.
4. Touch your chin to your chest.
5. Feel the tightness in your neck.

Hands and Arms

1. Make a fist with your right hand.
2. Feel the tension in your hands and fingers.
3. Now let those muscles go; let them relax.
4. Press your right elbow against the arm of the chair.

Face and Head

1. Tense the muscles of your lower jaw by pulling your lips back toward your ears as far as they will go.
2. Notice the tension.
3. Now relax those muscles totally; just let them go.
4. Tense the muscles of your lips and around your mouth by pursing your lips hard.

13. Feel the tension again.
14. Now return to your normal position and let those muscles relax.
15. Tighten the muscles of your upper back by trying to touch your shoulders together behind you.
16. Feel the tension in your upper back.
17. Let those muscles relax.

6. Now return to your normal position and just let those muscles go; let them relax.
7. Drop your head back until it touches your shoulders, and hold it there.
8. Feel the tension in the back of your neck.
9. Relax these muscles totally.

5. Tense the muscles of your forearm and bicep.
6. Hold it; notice the tension.
7. Now let those muscles relax.
8. Repeat for the left hand and arm.

5. Notice the tension.
6. Now let them relax; let them go.
7. Tense the muscles around your eyes by clenching your eyes as tight as you can.
8. Notice the tension.
9. Relax those muscles as completely as you can.
10. Tense the muscles of your

eyes, forehead, and scalp by raising your eyebrows as high as you can.

11. Hold it; notice the tension.

12. Now just release that tension totally; just relax those muscles.

This exercise should be done at least once, and preferably twice, daily. At the end of a week, you should notice definite improvement in your ability to relax. You are ready to begin relaxing more general muscle groups.

Step 2: Relaxing General Muscle Groups. When you are confident in your ability to relax each specific muscle, you are ready to proceed to the six general muscle groups: (1) feet and legs, (2) buttocks and stomach, (3) chest and back, (4) shoulders and neck, (5) hands and arms, and (6) face and head.

The procedure for the general muscle groups is very straight-forward. Having become familiar with muscular tension through the first step, you will find you are able to tense each group of muscles relatively easily. Tense the muscle group for a count of 5, then simply let all the muscles in that group relax, much as you did with each specific muscle. While relaxing, count for at least twice as long as you did when tensing—count 10 if you tensed them for a count of 5, for example. Start with your feet and legs, then proceed up your body as you did in the first step. Remember to relax your muscles fully after each period of tensing.

Just before you relax your muscles, introduce a cue. This cue may be a word you say to yourself while picturing it in your mind's eye, a word like "CALM" or "RELAX"—whatever word you choose. This procedure, called cue-controlled relaxation, is a shorthand system for training your body to relax quickly.

After practicing this procedure for a week—or until you can go quickly and easily through the muscle groups—you are ready to practice relaxing your muscles without tensing them first. Tensing was simply a method of teaching you what muscular tension feels like and how to reduce it; now you can dispense with it.

Step 3: Relaxing the Whole Body on Cue. This next step is easy. Use your cue to let your whole body relax immediately. Then identify general or specific areas of remaining tension and relax them. Use this procedure throughout the day to reduce both general and specific muscular tension.

Step 4: Spot Tension Reduction. Having become proficient at iden-tifying muscular tension, you can begin paying attention to its presence throughout your daily life. Most likely you will find that specific situations or events trigger increased muscle tension. You will probably also find that you tend to tense one or several specific muscles or one or two general muscle groups. You can now use cue-controlled relaxation to relax these particular muscles or muscle groups.

Imagery-Induced Relaxation

People who are able to imagine vividly and easily can acquire the technique of imagery-induced relaxation much more rapidly than they can that of tensing and releasing. This technique also requires a quiet place and a comfortable chair. Though imagery can involve all five senses—sight, sound, smell, touch, and taste—most people can only include one or two senses readily. The more senses you involve in your imagery, the more involved your body will be in responding to the imagery; fortunately, the ability to imagine improves with practice and with freedom from distraction.

Distraction often comes from within, in the form of intrusive thoughts that need to be eliminated for you to fully engage in the scene you are imagining. If you have difficulty getting into an image, try the following:

1. Give yourself adequate time. Especially when you first begin practicing, you will require more time to get into a scene.
2. Let your body calm down somewhat by just sitting quietly for a few minutes before starting the imagery session.
3. Concentrate on the details of an image, aspects that you can examine closely and that make the scene more real.
4. Let the image come. Imagining is a passive technique; let the image happen to you. Once you have chosen what scene you will use to relax, let the scene direct you as if you were being taken on a tour of it.
5. When thoughts intrude, "distract the distractor" by paying more attention to the details of the imagined scene. If this does not work, follow the intruding thought; let it play itself out and then return to the imagined scene. This technique is best to use only when distracting the distractor fails. You may have to let the intrusive thought play itself out a number of times, especially when you first begin to apply this technique.

If imaging proves consistently difficult or if intrusive thoughts generate too much anxiety, you will probably have to use one of the other relaxation strategies.

Step 1. The first step in imagery-induced relaxation is to select a scene that you find very relaxing, usually from some idyllic time in your past when you were especially relaxed and at peace. The scene you select need be no more complicated than a quiet evening at home. The idea is to select a scene that you associate with feeling especially relaxed.

The following two examples present common themes:

1. *the beach:* Imagine the beach at your favorite time—unpopulated or crowded, morning or evening, summer or fall, the surf quiet or pounding. Imagine yourself there. *Feel* the sand against your feet. *Feel* the sun warming your body. *See* the waves as they roll to the shore. *Feel* the rhythm of the waves; let them relax you. *Smell* the ocean air. *Hear* the waves as they lap onto the shore. *Feel* your body relaxing as you become immersed in being here. Let it happen!

2. *the countryside:* Imagine yourself lying next to a stream in a field full of flowers. *Smell* the freshness of the day. *Feel* the warmth of the sun and the gentle breeze blowing across your face. *Listen* to the sounds of the countryside—the birds singing, the brook trickling over the rocks. *See* the clear water rolling past as you forget all your worries and just let yourself be surrounded by the wonder of the day.

Step 2. Place yourself in the scene you have chosen, and let the events of that scene wash over you. As in the descriptions above, feel the events happening to you. Involve as many senses as you can. The more deeply you can get into the scene, the richer your experience will be.

Step 3. Eliminate any part of the scene that detracts from your pleasure. Leave any worries at home. If the presence of children detracts, leave them with a relative. If the company of a spouse detracts, take the excursion alone. The scene is yours to create in whatever way brings you the most relaxing enjoyment.

Step 4. Practice the scene frequently, adding details or altering it if you get bored. As you practice, you will become more expert at eliminating intrusive thoughts and negative associations. You will be able to enter a relaxed state more quickly and with less effort.

Step 5. Apply the imagery technique in real-life situations. When you are stressed at work or at home, take five minutes to imagine your favorite scene. Your overall tension will drop, and you'll become more efficient. Your efficiency and problem-solving ability decrease when your level of tension and anxiety is high. Conversely, they improve when you are relaxed—but still alert.

Diaphragmatic Breathing

This approach is the most versatile of the three relaxation techniques. No quiet place or comfortable chair is required. You can practice it while you're driving a car or working at your desk, in a crowd of people or by yourself. You can use it as a way of reducing your body tension and anxiety in general, or you can use it to bring a panic attack under control.

As we discussed in Chapter 3, people commonly hyperventilate before panicking. People who hyperventilate may breathe through their mouths, take short shallow breaths, or sigh frequently. Diaphragmatic breathing slows your breathing down so that you don't hyperventilate and also helps you relax your body. During a panic attack, you may find it impossible to take a full, deep breath. Diaphragmatic breathing will help you to gain control of your breathing in these situations.

Take a couple of minutes to observe your breathing as you read this book. Does your stomach rise first as you inhale, with your chest rising afterward? If not, you are not breathing from your diaphragm.

Learning diaphragmatic breathing is relatively easy. Breathe through your nose during these exercises.

1. Breathing normally, count the number of breaths you take per minute. Your goal is to breathe, while at rest, between 9 and 16 times per minute.
2. Place your hand over your abdomen. When you inhale, your abdomen should rise first and your upper chest second. Practice breathing in this fashion, slowing your rate until you are breathing 9 to 16 times per minute.
3. Practice these steps twice daily for ten minutes. Also make a conscious effort to slow your breathing down and breathe from your diaphragm throughout the day. These exercises should prove especially helpful when your chest is feeling tight and when you feel as if you cannot get a full breath.

If diaphragmatic breathing does not enable you to get a full breath during a panic attack itself, you can use two other procedures. Remember that shortness of breath, called dyspnea, results from insufficient carbon dioxide in your blood. What causes your symptoms is not too little oxygen but too much oxygen. The remedy, accordingly, is to increase your carbon dioxide level. This can be done either by breathing into a paper bag or by exhaling as much as you can, exhaling even more, and then slowly inhaling—a procedure that you will need to repeat several times.

Armed with these three relaxation techniques—tensing and releasing, imagery-induced relaxation, and diaphragmatic breathing—you should be able to reduce your overall level of tension, short-circuit your panic attacks before they start, and limit their duration once they are underway.

Indirect Strategies

Sometimes the symptoms of the panic attack simply do not abate when you apply direct coping strategies. At these times, the most effective strategy may be to direct your attention elsewhere. Think of distraction techniques as ways of coping with your attack until it passes: that way, you are less likely to expect too much from them. This attitude will also help you rank your distraction strategies in terms of their effectiveness, their conspicuousness, and their relative difficulty in implementing.

You saw earlier in the chapter that distraction strategies fall into two groups—physical and passive, while cognitive distraction techniques were grouped with other cognitive strategies. Though all distraction techniques are in a sense cognitive, some rely on physical activities to shift your attention away from your symptoms, while others rely on cognitive or passive activities to do the same. Physical distractions also can be subdivided into two types—those that direct your attention to other things (distraction by other-involvement) —and those that provide sensory input that competes with the panic attack symptoms. Let's look at some examples of each of these groups.

Cognitive Distraction

Cognitive distraction simply involves thinking about things other than your panic symptoms. The imagery-induced relaxation technique described earlier is a cognitive distraction as well as a relaxation technique: it directs your attention internally to something else. Additional cognitive distraction techniques include:

- counting
- thinking of a song
- remembering an important event in your life
- having sexual fantasies
- thinking of a situation that arouses a competing emotion, such as happiness, satisfaction, or joy
- thinking of an event to which you are eagerly looking forward

Using a little self-knowledge and trial and error, you can best determine, which of these is likely to work best for you. Simply put—use what works!

Identify in advance what cognitive distractions you will use to cope with your next panic attack; that way, you'll be able to remind yourself to use the technique, and you'll know specifically what thoughts to address when you're actually feeling the panic symptoms.

Physical Distraction: Doing Something Else

A number of my clients have reported waking from a sound sleep in the midst of a panic attack. How do they cope with it? They may lie silently in bed trying not to disturb their partner. They may try to relax or use cognitive distraction techniques. They may try to figure out the source of their anxiety. Minutes may turn into hours, and their attack may or may not abate. If it continues, it wears them out and deprives them of needed sleep.

I ask such clients two questions: Can you identify a point where you know you won't be able to get the attack under control and return to sleep? Almost always they answer "Yes!"

Then why not get out of bed and do something else until the attack has subsided? I ask.

This question usually surprises them. People who wouldn't think twice about doing something else during any other panic attack are paralyzed when an attack happens during the night.

The same principles apply wherever you are. When the circumstances of your attack focus all of your attention on your symptoms and when other coping strategies fail to bring the attack under control, changing what you're doing will often assist you in getting control of your symptoms.

- Do some housework.
- Work on a hobby.
- If you're sitting, go for a walk.
- If you're inside, go outside.
- If it's quiet, turn on the television or listen to music.
- If you're in the kitchen, go into the den.
- If you're alone, go where there are people.

All of these actions, and the dozens more I'm sure you can identify, serve to distract you from your symptoms. That distraction accomplishes two things: it reduces the discomfort of the symptoms themselves, and it shortens the duration of the attack by breaking the feedback loop between your attention and your symptoms. Figure 5.1 depicts how distraction techniques break the vicious cycle of panic.

Physical Distraction: Feeling Something Else

The inventiveness of people with panic attacks never ceases to fascinate me. Panic sufferers are the absolutely best source for learning effective coping strategies. Some of my favorites are those used for sensory distraction. Here are a few examples.

Peter was having a panic attack at his in-laws' house one Christmas holiday. He tried several cognitive distraction and relaxation

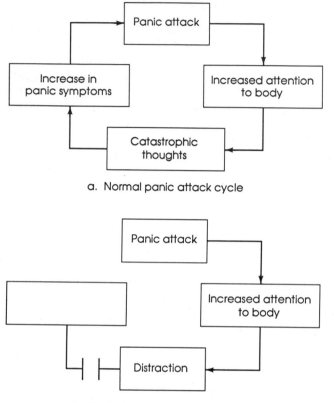

a. Normal panic attack cycle

b. Cycle broken through distraction

Figure 5.1 Breaking the panic cycle through distraction

techniques to no avail. Finally, he walked out in the snow in his bare feet. Within a minute, his panic attack stopped.

Another client stumbled onto something similar. Reeling from a panic attack of several hours' duration, Jim finally went outside into a warm summer night. Walking on his gravel driveway in his bare feet, he was surprised to find his symptoms diminish. He was then able to get further control by using some breathing exercises.

Another client, Joan, was awakened from her sleep with an attack. Thrashing around in bed, she woke up her husband, who asked if he could do anything. She asked him to make love to her. The panic attack was over in minutes.

I have known people who:

- rub various parts of their bodies
- take hot or cold baths or showers
- go for walks in the rain

- pinch themselves
- exercise

All of these approaches have one thing in common: they provide tactile sensory input to compete with the physical sensations experienced during panic attacks. Like all distraction techniques, they also shift the person's attention away from his or her panic symptoms. If the sensory input is intense enough, this approach can—and often does—totally eliminate the panic symptoms. Its principal drawback is that finding or producing competing sensory stimulation is not always easy when a panic attack is occurring. Nonetheless, it is an excellent strategy to have in one's coping repertoire.

Communicating with Others

Seeking help or simply communicating is basically another form of distraction. Because it combines distraction with some additional coping features, however, it deserves special attention.

Have you ever had a panic attack and, thinking it a heart attack or the like, rushed to the emergency room of your local hospital, only to have all of your symptoms disappear before you saw the doctor? Or have you ever called a health care provider while having a prolonged panic attack, only to find your symptoms abate while you were talking to her? Numerous times, I've seen the symptoms of panic evaporate before my eyes or heard them abate over a phone simply because the person was talking to someone. Moreover, people who experience panic attacks consistently report that human contact is one of the best ways to reduce or even stop an attack.

Why then do people who suffer panic attacks or the professionals who treat them not consider talking to someone a coping strategy? Why, further, do both sufferers and professionals alike often frown on talking to someone? Because it has such potential for abuse. Let's look at some examples:

- A woman calls her husband home from work every time she has a panic attack.
- A man calls his psychologist every time his panic attacks last longer than five minutes.
- A woman has visited the Emergency Room 20 times in the last month because she thought she was having a stroke.
- A man will enter stores and restaurants only if his wife accompanies him.

Clearly, the potential for abusing relationships, overspending on health care, prolonging dependent relationships, and avoiding dealing with one's fears is high. On the other hand, consider the following examples of an irrational failure to use relationships to better cope with panic:

- Mary is attending a dinner party when she begins experiencing the symptoms of a panic attack. Afraid to tell anyone she is feeling bad and afraid to leave the table, she continues to suffer through the meal. As she feels more and more trapped, her symptoms escalate.
- John is afraid that his panic symptoms mean that he is crazy. He, of course, concludes that anyone else who knew of his symptoms would also conclude he was crazy. Accordingly, he keeps his attacks secret from his wife, friends, and physician. His self-imposed silence reinforces his belief in his craziness, and his symptoms escalate.

A middle ground between the two extremes appears to be desirable, but where do we draw the line? Let's consider some guidelines:

1. Do not abuse personal or professional relationships. One way to avoid abusing personal relationships is to work out in advance what you would like from someone and what he or she is willing to give you. The same approach should be used in dealing with professionals. Discuss in advance what kind and how much communication they will accept should you experience a severe panic attack. These kinds of contingencies can be especially important in the early phase of treatment, when your attacks are still frequent.

2. Don't view the communication as a means of rescue but rather as a way for you to cope with your attacks. Both you and the person you are involving should understand clearly that you don't expect him or her to make the attack go away. Further, unless he or she is a health care professional, you can't expect the person to fill a professional's role by diagnosing your condition. Tell your supporter that what you want is a listener whom you can tell what you are experiencing, and perhaps someone to hold your hand or hug you if that helps you feel better.

3. If you tell your friends, be simple and direct. Do not explain what is happening in catastrophic terms that are likely to alarm them. If they know that you are not in danger and that you need only to be able to state how you are feeling, they are more likely to be helpful. After all, how helpful could you be if someone informed you he was having a stroke and demanded assistance?

The Strategy of Letting the Attack Happen

The strategy of letting the attack happen does not fall into any of the preceding coping groups. This strategy refers to taking an accepting·

attitude toward your attack—waiting for it to end rather than trying to force it to end. The strategy of letting the attack happen may at first appear to contradict the purpose of coping strategies—that is, to mitigate your attacks. Properly understood, however, it is anything but contradictory.

Effective coping strategies are not frantic attempts to eliminate your panic attacks. They are reasoned approaches to reducing your attacks with the goal of *eventually* eliminating them. This nonfrantic attitude is essential to successfully using coping strategies. Letting the attack happen does not mean doing nothing to reduce your symptoms. It does mean taking an observer's stance to see if the techniques you are using are working. The first benefit of this strategy is that it allows you to employ other strategies more effectively.

Letting the attack happen can be beneficial in a second way. If an attack continues for an extended period of time (more than an hour, for example) in spite of your using a number of strategies to try to cope with it, taking a passive attitude toward the attack has the therapeutic value of not fueling the attack with worrisome thoughts about when it will stop. A passive attitude will also promote relaxation and allow whatever other coping strategies you are using to be more effective. In a later chapter on strategies for coping with catastrophic thinking, we will discuss how to deal with some of the thoughts that arise during a prolonged panic attack.

Although many panic sufferers use the coping strategies in groups G and H, they are really counterproductive. Applying the guidelines we developed in the previous chapter for identifying bad coping strategies, we can see that bodily abuse and avoidance have several negative consequences: (1) they don't work over the long run, (2) they reduce your sense of self-efficacy, and (3) they reduce your self-esteem.

Summary

In this chapter we examined coping strategies—some of which you may already use and some of which you may not. We also discussed in some detail the specifics of several successful coping strategies. These strategies work to reduce the symptoms of panic as well as anxiety and tension, which increase your vulnerability to panic attacks.

You should be able to identify and apply the following strategies:

1. Know and be able to remind yourself what a panic attack is and that what you are having is a panic attack.
2. Determine what circumstances have led to particular attacks.
3. Distinguish your symptoms of panic from your thoughts about those symptoms.

4. Relax your muscles using either the tensing and releasing or the imagery-induced relaxation technique.
5. Know how to spot the effects of hyperventilation and how to combat these effects with proper breathing techniques.
6. Know the three basic methods of distraction and when to employ them.
7. Know when and how to utilize other people in coping with your attacks.
8. When you have done whatever you can to cope with a panic attack and it persists, just let the attack happen.

Panic Thinking:
Catastrophic Cognitions

As many as 1 out of every 3 adults will have a panic attack this year. Yet no more than 1 out of 50 will develop a panic disorder. What accounts for this fact? Why are some people able to shrug off a panic attack and go on with their lives while others become traumatized by their attacks, sometimes to the point of never leaving their homes?

Many people who experience the physical symptoms of panic would not even consider themselves to have had a panic attack. Yet their heart rates and respiration have increased, their hands and feet have numbed, and they report having felt strange, as if they or the world were unreal. Many people who have such symptoms are simply not particularly bothered by them. They never visit an emergency room. They consult no specialists and undergo no expensive diagnostic procedures. They may never report the events to their personal physicians. Only when panic attack symptoms are described to them are they able to say, "Hey, I have those!"

Which One Are You?

Since you're reading this book, chances are you're not such a person; rather than dispassionately accepting your panic symptoms you've probably wondered anxiously what was happening to you. How people answer the question "What is happening to me?" accounts in large part for why some people develop panic disorder and others don't.

The simple fact is that, though your attacks originate in physical symptoms, your thoughts about those symptoms are the basis for (1) your attacks getting worse; (2) your attacks becoming frequent; (3) your terror itself; (4) your avoidance of situations that you associate with attacks; and (5) the disorder spiraling downward, with your attacks, terror, and avoidance increasingly worsening. If you compare the overall effects of your symptoms to the overall effects of your thoughts about the symptoms, you can see that the thoughts, by far, cause the greater disability.

Consider Figure 6.1. Person A's catastrophic interpretation of symptoms leads to maladaptive coping strategies, while Person B's interpretation of the same symptoms leads to adaptive coping.

Some of the most destructive interpretations of panic symptoms involve the belief that one is going crazy. Such a belief often leads people to avoid public situations, because associated with the notion of going crazy are a number of inaccurate and exaggerated fears: of losing control and behaving bizarrely, even violently, or of wandering around totally unaware of your actions.

At the very least, catastrophic thinking heightens your level of arousal both during and after an attack. During an attack, this heightened arousal exacerbates your panic symptoms. After an attack, this heightened arousal causes you to become hypervigilant in looking for symptoms you associate with panic attacks. As we have already seen, such hypervigilance inevitably increases the likelihood of further attacks.

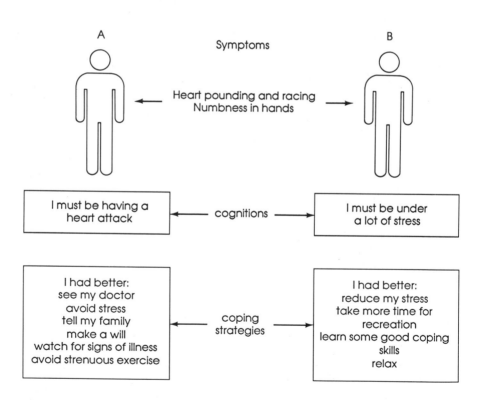

Figure 6.1 How cognitions affect coping strategies

Let's examine in more careful detail the impact of cognitions on panic attacks.

How Catastrophic Is Your Thinking?

What do you think during a panic attack? After an attack? The Panic Attack Cognitions Questionnaire (PACQ) was developed at the Anxiety Disorders Clinic to measure what people with panic attacks think both during and after attacks. The thoughts listed in the PACQ were identified through my therapeutic work with panic attack sufferers who were asked to list thoughts they had during and after panic attacks. You can find out how catastrophically you think during and after panic by answering the questionnaire presented in Table 6.1.

The questionnaire yields two scores: one for your thoughts during an attack and one for your thoughts after an attack. To obtain your scores, simply total your points for each of the two columns. Your score for the first column—your thoughts during an attack—is more important than your second score, as it is this first set of thoughts that causes your panic symptoms to escalate during an attack. Your postattack thoughts—represented by your total for the second column—relate to your anticipation of future attacks and the worry associated with that anticipation.

After obtaining your two scores, you can use the scale given below to compare the severity of your catastrophic cognitions with that of other panic sufferers. The scale ranks only your thoughts during an attack—your first score—primarily because your thoughts during an attack provide the best basis for estimating the severity of your attacks relative to other panic sufferers.

Severe = 69 or higher. 7% of panic sufferers have this many catastrophic cognitions in this range.

Marked = 57–68. 24% of panic sufferers have catastrophic cognitions in this range.

Average = 44–56. 38% of panic sufferers have catastrophic cognitions in this range.

Low = 32–43. 24% of panic sufferers have catastrophic cognitions in this range.

Very Low = 25–31. 7% of panic sufferers have catastrophic cognitions in this range.

One of your goals should be to reduce your catastrophic cognitions to at least a low level. If your attacks are already mild in terms of your thoughts, one of the goals of your treatment should be to eliminate your catastrophic cognitions.

Table 6.1   Panic Attack Cognitions Questionnaire

Instructions: Frightening thoughts often accompany or follow panic attacks. Think of your last panic attack. Using the scale below, rate each of the following thoughts according to the degree to which you thought it during and after this panic attack. Remember to rate each thought twice, once for during and once for after your last attack.

1 = not at all; 2 = some, but not much; 3 = quite a lot; 4 = totally dominated your thoughts

						During	*After*
1. I am going to die.	1	2	3	4		1	1
2. I am going insane.	1	2	3	4		2	2
3. I am losing control.	1	2	3	4		4	1
4. This will never end.	1	2	3	4		3	2
5. I am really scared.	1	2	3	4		2	1
6. I am having a heart attack.	1	2	3	4		1	1
7. I am going to pass out.	1	2	3	4		1	1
8. I don't know what people will think	1	2	3	4		2	1
9. I won't be able to get out of here.	1	2	3	4		3	2
10. I don't understand what is happening to me.	1	2	3	4		3	2
11. People will think I am crazy.	1	2	3	4		2	1
12. I will always be this way.	1	2	3	4		4	2
13. I am going to throw up.	1	2	3	4		3	1
14. I must have a brain tumor.	1	2	3	4		1	1
15. I will choke to death.	1	2	3	4		1	1
16. I am going to act foolish.	1	2	3	4		1	1
17. I am going blind.	1	2	3	4		1	1
18. I will hurt someone.	1	2	3	4		2	1
19. I am going to have a stroke.	1	2	3	4		1	1
20. I am going to scream.	1	2	3	4		2	1
21. I am going to babble or talk funny.	1	2	3	4		1	1
22. I will be paralyzed by fear.	1	2	3	4		2	1
23. Something is really physically wrong with me.	1	2	3	4		1	1
24. I will not be able to breathe.	1	2	3	4		1	1
25. Something terrible will happen.	1	2	3	4		2	1

44   30

Classifying Your Catastrophic Cognitions

As with your panic symptoms, your catastrophic cognitions may be grouped in clusters that represent the kind of cognitions you have. These clusters consist of the following:

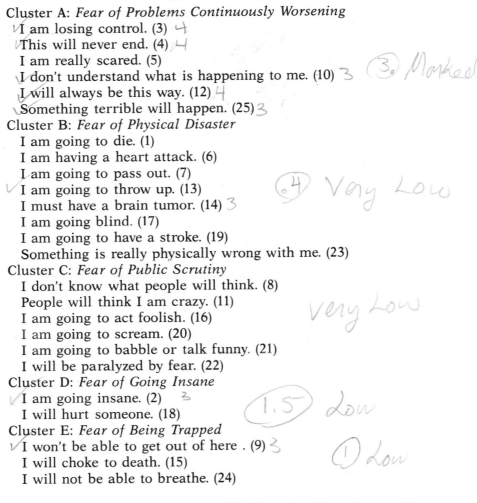

Cluster A: *Fear of Problems Continuously Worsening*
  ✓I am losing control. (3) 4
  ✓This will never end. (4) 4
  I am really scared. (5)
  ✓I don't understand what is happening to me. (10) 3 ③. *Marked*
  ✓I will always be this way. (12) 4
  ✓Something terrible will happen. (25) 3
Cluster B: *Fear of Physical Disaster*
  I am going to die. (1)
  I am having a heart attack. (6)
  I am going to pass out. (7)
  ✓I am going to throw up. (13)   ⓪.4 *Very Low*
  I must have a brain tumor. (14) 3
  I am going blind. (17)
  I am going to have a stroke. (19)
  Something is really physically wrong with me. (23)
Cluster C: *Fear of Public Scrutiny*
  I don't know what people will think. (8)
  People will think I am crazy. (11)
  I am going to act foolish. (16)   *very Low*
  I am going to scream. (20)
  I am going to babble or talk funny. (21)
  I will be paralyzed by fear. (22)
Cluster D: *Fear of Going Insane*
  ✓I am going insane. (2)   3
  I will hurt someone. (18)   ①.5 *Low*
Cluster E: *Fear of Being Trapped*
  ✓I won't be able to get out of here . (9) 3
  I will choke to death. (15)   ① *Low*
  I will not be able to breathe. (24)

You can see that the PACQ comprises five cognitive clusters. You can get your average score for each cluster by adding up your score for each item in the cluster and dividing by the number of items in each cluster. For your convenience, each item is followed by a parenthetical number corresponding to its number on the PACQ. Compare your score for each cluster with the following scale:

Severe = 3.5–4.0
Marked = 2.5–3.5

Average = 1.5–2.5
Low = 1.0–1.5
Very Low = 0–1.0

Your cognitive cluster scores will help you identify how you interpret the symptoms you are experiencing. Notice that two kinds of cognitions make up the PACQ. One is an interpretation or explanation of what is happening during the attack—what I term an *attribution*. The other is a *prediction* of what is going to happen. We'll first examine these attributions and predictions, and then we'll examine how and why they develop.

Mistaken Attributions: The Core of Catastrophic Thinking

An attribution is an explanation of why something is happening, has happened, or has failed to happen. A mistaken attribution, then, is an incorrect explanation of why something has happened or failed to happen. The explanation may be plausible, but it is wrong.

Superstitions, for example, are mistaken attributions. A black cat crosses your path. Sometime later you trip and scrape your knee. You attribute your fall to the bad luck caused by the black cat's crossing your path.

A large body of psychological research demonstrates that mistaken attributions are a primary factor in the development of depression. People who become depressed are more likely to blame themselves and assume total responsibility for any negative event, regardless of whether or not such attributions make sense.

A different pattern of attributions characterizes panic disorder. Instead of attributing your symptoms to some personal failing, you attribute them to some catastrophic event or illness.

Why is your heart pounding? Because you have heart disease and are having a heart attack!

Why are your hands feeling numb and disconnected from your body? Because you are going crazy!

Such attributions are incorrect, yet can prove stubbornly resistant to change even when you learn the correct explanation for your symptoms. One reason for this is that the correct explanation is often supplied tentatively: "It may be that you're having panic attacks," or "I'm not sure , but I think you're having panic attacks." Information given in this way is unlikely to alter your original attributions. You will continue to believe that you're having a heart attack or going crazy. Medical and psychological experts may fail to allay your concerns because their explanations tend to be incomplete and offered without providing you an opportunity to explore your own concerns and thoughts regarding what is happening to you.

Inaccurate Predictions

Inaccurate attributions usually also mean inaccurate predictions about what your symptoms will lead to. Some common predictions include:

- I will pass out.
- I will go crazy.
- I will babble or talk funny.
- I will have a heart attack.
- I will not know what I am doing.

The interesting thing about these predictions is that they appear to be irrefutable. They are not understood to be predictions, nor are they located in time. Compare the examples above with:

- I will pass out at least once during one of my next five attacks.
- I will go crazy if these attacks last a month.

Notice that, like many apocalyptic predictions, catastrophic predictions include no time limit. Panic sufferers who have been having attacks for years persist in predicting that they will soon lapse into total insanity, in spite of their continuing—or at least, apparent—sanity.

How do such thoughts develop? Are they random; that is, are you just as likely to develop one set of thoughts as another? Or do they make sense in some way?

Symptoms and Cognitions

Since catastrophic attributions are attempts to explain the symptoms you are experiencing, they directly relate to the kinds of physical symptoms you are experiencing. Thus:

- If your body or surroundings feel strange, you are likely to conclude that you're going insane.
- If your hands or feet feel numb or tingly, you're likely to think you're having a heart attack or stroke.
- If you have chest pain or your heart is beating rapidly, you're also likely to suspect a heart attack.

Inaccurate predictions are likewise related to the type of symptoms you are experiencing:

- If you're feeling nauseated, you may predict that you're about to lose control.
- If you're feeling dizzy or light-headed, you may predict that you will faint.
- If you're feeling disconnected from your own body or your environment, you may predict that your condition will worsen and you won't know who you are or what you are doing.

Mistaken ideas about how or why things happen—attributions— can directly lead to inaccurate predictions about whether or not things will happen. One woman I was treating believed that the stress produced by fearing she would have a heart attack would cause a heart attack to happen—perfectly circular reasoning. She summed up her thinking on the subject thusly: "Stress can produce heart attacks, you know."

Even catastrophic thoughts have a basis in reason, however. You are trying to explain feelings that are strange and painful to you, and you arrive at certain interpretations because whatever information you have indicates that that is what the symptoms *may* mean. When these initial interpretations do not yield to additional information and alternative explanations, they become problematic, however.

We will now examine some of the factors that contribute to catastrophic thinking.

The Soil that Produces Panic

Lack of Information

People who attribute their panic symptoms to catastrophe typically lack information that would allow them to correctly label their experience. Before 1980, when panic disorder was officially defined in the DSM-III, public health professionals did not recognize this experience. Though anxiety states were known to exist, they were not recognized as discrete, unique phenomena. With mental health experts unaware of the problem, the general public had no way of labeling their experience accurately.

Because panic disorders had not been named, they had not been studied. Consequently, no information on their frequency and severity was available. Their relationship to other disorders, both physical and mental, was largely unknown. The course panic disorders took, whether improving or worsening, was likewise unknown. Individuals experiencing panic attacks thus suffered them within a vacuum of information.

Without a name to attach to it, subjective experience can be baffling. Rather than trying to understand the experience on its own terms, you are likely to try to fit it in with what you already know. The event of panic is no different. Its abrupt onset and its disruptiveness demand that you attach some meaning to it. What meaning you attach will depend largely on the information you have as well as on your personal history.

Action Is Information

That your behavior greatly influences your attitudes is axiomatic. The psychological theory of *cognitive dissonance* explains this influence. According to this theory, deciding to behave in a particular way biases your attitudes toward that decision. Take, for example, a person who has not eaten for a day. In spite of her hunger, if she decides to fast an additional day, she will perceive herself to be less hungry after her decision than before it.

Now take a person who has a panic attack in a restaurant. After appraising his condition, he decides to leave the restaurant. This action is almost always interpreted as "I felt so bad I had to leave!" Notice the two thoughts derived from the action of leaving: "I felt so bad," and "I had to leave." Forgotten is the fact that he made a decision. He, like many people, will conclude that the restaurant *caused* the attack. Now imagine this same person deciding to see a series of medical specialists, endure a number of diagnostic tests, take a variety of medications, and enter a hospital. The information being communicated in this series of decisions is that his problem with panic attacks is so bad that all of these actions are warranted.

Similarly, a decision to stay in the restaurant is also information. The information conveyed in this case is "The panic attack wasn't so bad; I was able to stay and finish my meal." Deciding not to submit to a variety of diagnostic tests *after prudent counsel* is also information. Deciding to base your treatment on the most likely diagnosis, and not the least likely, conveys to you, "I have a panic disorder. A brain tumor is unlikely." What action you take thus largely determines what your thoughts will be.

The Actions of Others

Not only do your decisions and your actions influence your thoughts, but so do the actions of those around you. Contrast a friend's or relative's cool, calm, and collected response to one of your panic attacks with a frantic, fearful response. Someone who has you sit down and breathe slowly while he or she holds your hand conveys the information that what you are experiencing is neither frightening nor beyond your ability to deal with. Someone who concludes that you may be having a heart attack and whisks you off to the hospital communicates an unconscious message that is difficult to shake. In your own state of anxiety and confusion, such external information can be not only powerful but decisive in determining how you interpret future panic attacks.

Once you have received a negative response or series of responses, of course, you cannot alter the past. Becoming aware of the influence such responses have on your interpretation of panic, however, enables you to do something about it. The first thing you can do is to tell the person how his or her response affects you. The second thing you can do is to instruct the person how to respond more appropriately. He or she will doubtless be happy to learn that you are not about to expire or enter the twilight zone when you're having a panic attack. Further, he or she will be happy to learn how best to assist you in dealing with the problem. No one likes to feel helpless, and that includes the people around you.

When others' actions express support along with a recognition of your ability to deal effectively with your panic or, at worst, to wait it out, your own thoughts are more likely to reflect such an attitude. You may wonder why you need others to respond appropriately to you. You may think, "If I'm able to tell other people how to respond to me, I shouldn't even need their support." The fact is, however, that you are much more likely to be able to think rationally about your attacks *between* attacks than you are *during* an attack. How others respond during an attack affects you significantly, and preparing them to respond at these times in a way most helpful to you is another effective coping strategy for you.

What kind of instructions might you give someone? Essentially, the same kind you would give yourself. Some examples:

- "If I'm panicking, realize that there's nothing physically or mentally wrong with me. I'm not going to die or go crazy."
- "Do not take me to the emergency room or call the rescue squad."
- "If we're in a restaurant or other such place where I might feel trapped, talk me through an attack without leaving. If I need to leave, encourage me to return once I've got my symptoms under control."
- "Help me arrive at my own understanding of what is happening, then help me identify how I want to cope with the attack."

Experience Is Information

Some people bring powerful experiences with death to their first experience of a panic attack. Joanna had nursed her husband through

the final stages of emphysema. Nightly, she would listen to him struggling to breathe, wondering if the next breath would be the one he
would be unable to take. Eventually, what she had feared and anticipated happened: he died in a quiet struggle to breathe. Later, when
Joanna's first panic attack came in the middle of the night and she
found herself unable to take a full breath, she naturally wondered if
this struggle to breathe would end in her own death. She knew, of
course, that she did not have emphysema, but she didn't know whether
or not she had some other equally dreadful illness. Her experience
with her husband determined how she would interpret her own
symptoms.

Other people bring vague fears to their first experience with panic.
Mark was one such person. An inveterate film-goer, he had recently
seen a movie in which a deranged man stabbed himself while in a psy-
chotic state. This image haunted him from time to time, and he wondered actively if he was capable of losing control and behaving
similarly. His first panic attack was dominated by a feeling of depersonalization that he described as a "dreamlike state in which the world
appeared as if seen through gauze." It immediately occurred to him
that he was no longer in control of his mind or body, a thought that
prompted the further association of the man stabbing himself with
a knife. He was making both an inaccurate attribution—that his
dreamlike state was caused by an underlying psychosis—and an inaccurate prediction—that this psychosis would lead him to stab
himself.

Such examples are common. In the absence of sufficient accurate
information, each person will come up with attributions and predictions based primarily on his or her personal history and fears.

Hypervigilance and Panic

Hypervigilance, the nearly constant scrutiny of your body for evidence
that a panic attack is about to erupt, is primarily a cognitive process
in which any and all physical aberrations, and many normal events,
are construed as abnormal. It is a process in which you are constantly
asking, "Am I okay?" "Is anything wrong with me?" "What does it
mean that I'm feeling hot, or tired, or tense, or whatever?" The hypervigilant person frequently monitors his or her body. He may take his
pulse regularly or when he feels threatened. She may listen carefully
for skipped heartbeats or pauses between heartbeats. He may constantly test his ability to swallow or to take a full breath.

If you seek, you're likely to find. Fluctuations in your body's functioning are not unusual; the vast majority of these fluctuations are
normal and no cause for concern. But if you are looking for aberra-

tions, you will interpret normal variations as aberrant. This is the case when, feeling dizzy after getting up quickly from a reclining position—and thereby inducing a temporary state of light-headedness—you conclude that you're going to pass out or have a panic attack. This is the case when you enter a hot room, feel hot, and conclude that you're in the first phase of a panic attack. If you are mentally set to find disorder, you will interpret information accordingly.

Hypervigilance is also associated with the cognitive cluster of fearing public scrutiny, usually based on the mistaken belief that people are more critical of you than is actually the case. Hypervigilance in this case is almost totally a cognitive process. The person who chronically fears public embarrassment already feels embarrassed. Expecting the worst, you turn your hypervigilance inward and conclude that because you feel ashamed and embarrassed, someone is being critical of you. Of course, this connection between your embarrassment and the assumption that someone has noticed you in a vulnerable posture is seldom made consciously. Prepared by your belief system to expect criticism you will interpret any act, however small, by anyone you think has noticed your shortcomings as evidence of the offense.

Hypervigilance in this case is selective. Your aim is to detect any information that supports your assumption. Simultaneously, however, you selectively screen out incoming information which is inconsistent with your preconceptions. This process is frequently apparent in individuals who are characteristically shy and anxious in social settings. It is also apparent in individuals who have developed a panic disorder. Because your internal experience of a panic attack is so powerful, you come to expect that your experience is being manifested externally. Since no one likes to be seen as weak or sick, people often immediately respond with embarrassment—which then colors their experience of panic. People stop vigilantly pursuing evidence that they are about to be found out when their panic attacks themselves stop.

Hypochondriasis

Sometimes your attributions regarding what is happening to you become extreme. In spite of all evidence to the contrary, you persist in believing that you are suffering from a life-threatening illness. When this belief does not yield to consistent expert opinion, you are suffering from a condition called *hypochondriasis*. Panic disorder victims are often found to be somewhat hypochondriacal because they become overly attentive to their bodies and consistently misinterpret normal sensations and events as evidence of disease. Sometimes, this concern develops into a belief system and does not change regardless of evidence to the contrary. One of my clients, a woman named Martha, was convinced she had AIDS (acquired immune deficiency syndrome). Martha, who was married, had had a casual sexual relationship with a man she met at a convention. She felt guilty and depressed about this episode, which she insisted was her first casual sexual encounter. Upon returning home, she began to wonder what kind of man would engage in such activities. Thinking that he would most likely be promiscuous, she concluded that he might be carrying the AIDS virus. She immediately began to worry that she herself might be infected and instituted a number of precautionary measures: (1) she stopped having sexual relations with her husband, (2) she saw a doctor and was tested for the presence of the AIDS virus, and (3) she isolated herself when she or one of her family had a cut and while she was menstruating. In addition, Martha began looking for evidence that she was infected with the virus. When her hair came out when she brushed it, she associated the hair loss with cancer and took it as evidence that she had AIDS. When her gums bled when she brushed her teeth, she took this as evidence of the progression of the disease. When she caught a cold, it was proof positive of the failure of her immune system.

Her preoccupation with her belief that she was dying of AIDS grew, and her ability to function at home and at work declined. In the period of one year, she had six tests for the AIDS antibodies, all of which were negative. She was then sent to me and diagnosed as having hypochondriasis.

This preoccupation with her body produced a chronic state of tension and anxiety in Martha, which eventually erupted as panic attacks. Consistent with her belief that she was dying, Martha immediately construed her panic symptoms as further evidence that she was suffering some dread physical scourge.

Hypochondriasis markedly complicates the panic picture. There are two reasons for this, both of which are remediable:

1. Hypochondriasis produces a chronic state of tension and anxiety. While similar in many ways to tension and anxiety produced by conflict and acute stress, this state is also different. The sufferer is faced with the constant preoccupation that he or she has a debilitating or deadly disease.
2. Hypochondriasis produces a state of near-constant hypervigilance. The affected person has learned to monitor his or her body for every variation. When panic attacks develop, he has a ready-made cognitive system for making the meaning of his symptoms catastrophic.

Like panic attacks, hypochondriasis can be helped with techniques like those described in this book. Correction of this strongly entrenched attributional system, however, most often requires professional intervention.

The Panic Information Bundle

Everything that happens to you or around you when you are having a panic attack is stored together as an information bundle. The more elements from this bundle that are present in any situation, the higher your chances of reexperiencing a panic attack are. Further, other behaviors that are not part of the attack itself but that result from it, such as leaving a checkout line, are also more likely to occur as the number of elements that were present during earlier attacks increases. We have seen that symptoms, cognitions, and avoidance behaviors are all part of the events of a panic attack. So too are the situational cues that are present when an attack occurs. If you encounter a number of these four informational elements at a later time, you are likely to have another panic attack. For example, the following elements were present when David had his first panic attack:

1. He was in a restaurant.
2. The restaurant was crowded.
3. He was sitting away from the entrance.
4. He was with three business associates.
5. His first symptom was feeling hot, followed by nausea, dizziness, and blurred vision.
6. He thought he was going to throw up and embarrass himself.
7. He excused himself to go to the rest room.
8. He returned to his table and suffered through the meal.

The number of these elements that are present the next time David enters a restaurant will determine in part whether or not he has another full panic response. If he is with his wife and the restaurant is uncrowded, he is unlikely to expect a panic attack. If something should remind him of an occasion when he felt nauseated and threw up, the cognitive elements associated with David's first attack, combined with his being in a restaurant, would increase his chances of having another attack. By increasing the probability that David will recall his panic attack, the juxtaposition of these various elements also increases the probability that he will have another panic attack. It is as if the memory of the attack and the attack are interchangeable.

The information bundle may be triggered when the person experiences the same symptoms or catastrophic cognitions that accompanied an earlier attack or when he or she is in the physical setting where the attack occurred. *Any* of the elements of the attack are capable of eliciting *any* of the other elements. The symptom of feeling hot in a restaurant might elicit both the symptom of nausea and the thought of throwing up in front of a group of people. The thought of throwing up could likewise produce the symptoms of feeling hot and nauseated.

This property of panic attacks helps explain a couple of interesting characteristics of panic. The first is the tendency for panic attack sufferers to reexperience symptoms that they are describing or that others are talking about—the problem of contagion mentioned in Chapter 3. The second is reflected in the oft-heard refrain from panic victims that to say they're able to think logically through an attack is nice, but thinking logically when they're actually having that attack is another matter. This statement reflects the recognition that other thoughts and actions are "automatically" linked to their panic symptoms and that replacing automatic thoughts with logical thoughts can be a difficult task. As you practice techniques to cope with your attacks, you must recognize that all the information about an attack is being stored together. As you practice new coping responses in the context of the informational bundle (a technique described in detail in Chapter 8), you essentially replace the elements of the bundle with new elements.

Knowing about the informational bundle will help you to identify it when you encounter its effects.

Summary

Let's review what you have learned in this chapter:

1. Though panic attacks originate in physical symptoms, your thoughts about those symptoms are what cause your attacks to escalate. Catastrophic thoughts also lead to one of the most problematic consequences of panic: avoidance behavior.
2. Mistaken attributions—incorrect explanations for what you are experiencing—are at the core of catastrophic thinking and often give rise to inaccurate predictions about what your symptoms will lead to.
3. The principal factors contributing to catastrophic thinking are ignorance, your own responses to your panic, others' responses, and your past experiences with similar events.
4. Hypervigilance is primarily a cognitive process in which you interpret even normal variations in body functions as aberrant and as evidence of an ensuing panic attack.
5. Your symptoms, thoughts, and behavior, along with any situational cues that are present during an attack, all combine to form an information bundle. The presence of any of the elements of the information bundle can elicit any other element, and the more elements from the bundle that are present at any one time, the more likely you will be to have another panic attack.

7

Coping with
Catastrophic Cognitions

*E*vidence is accumulating to show that the ability to disarm catastrophic thinking is central to the successful treatment of panic. Research has shown that catastrophic thoughts both trigger panic attacks and exacerbate those already in progress. It makes sense that gaining control over those thoughts and changing them will stop a number of attacks from happening and reduce the severity and duration of others. Therapies that teach new ways to cognitively appraise panic symptoms are among the most successful in treating this problem. In this chapter, you'll learn strategies to change the catastrophic thoughts that breed panic to the positive thoughts that breed confidence.

Identifying the Connections Between Your Thoughts and Symptoms

As we discussed in Chapter 6, many people who suffer from panic disorder interpret their physical symptoms catastrophically. They then respond to their symptoms as if their interpretation were the reality. Before you can change this misinterpretation, you must first understand the connection you are making between your thoughts and your symptoms.

Separating Your Thoughts from Your Symptoms

To achieve this understanding, you must first record your experience. One of the best ways to do this is to reproduce your panic symptoms by imagining them and then describe your experience and your thoughts while speaking into a tape recorder. Another way to record your experience is to write down your symptoms the same way you would describe them to a doctor. Once you have recorded—either on tape or in writing—both your symptoms and your thoughts about them, the next step is to delineate clearly which are symptoms and which are thoughts. This step is important. Recognizing that the two are distinct allows you to treat them differently. Symptoms demand different coping strategies than do thoughts. A second benefit of distinguishing between the two is that the symptoms will become less threatening as you separate them from your interpretation of them.

Let's take an example. Asked to describe what symptoms he experienced during a panic attack, Ralph reported feeling as though he were suffocating, choking to death, and paralyzed. He was taught to separate his symptoms and thoughts as follows:

Symptoms	Thoughts
Can't get a full breath	I'm suffocating.
Chest is tight	I'm suffocating.
Mouth and throat are dry	I'm choking to death.
Throat muscles are tense	I'm choking to death.
Feet and arms are numb	I'm paralyzed.
Leg and arm muscles are tense	I'm paralyzed.

By drawing up these two lists, Ralph learned to distinguish which parts of his experience were physical sensations and which were thoughts he had about the physical sensations.

Simply recognizing that thoughts are different from symptoms is insufficient to gain mastery at making this distinction; you must practice distinguishing them. Here are several recommendations:

1. On a 3-by-5-inch card, write down your symptoms and the thoughts you associate with them. Rehearse differentiating these throughout the day.
2. Bring this card out during a panic attack. It will help remind you of the distinctions you need to make.
3. Practice separating your symptoms and cognitions while actually experiencing some of the symptoms.

Identifying the Connections Between Your Thoughts and Situations

You can also identify thoughts that you associate with specific situations or circumstances related to your panic attacks—specific places you associate with panic attacks, such as cars, checkout lines, and so on, or environmental circumstances, such as a hot room, a crowded store, or driving alone. Identifying these links is a first step toward breaking them.

Ask yourself, "What do I fear will happen if I go into that place or enter that situation?" Follow that question up with, "What do I fear will happen next?" Keep asking and answering that question until you can go no further. Write down all of your answers so that you will know precisely what you are afraid of in these situations.

Use the form in Table 7.1 to identify your thoughts about feared situations.

Separating Your Thoughts from Situations

Now look at Table 7.2. This form was completed by a patient named Irene. Notice that the two situations Irene associated with panic both

Table 7.1 Identifying Your Thoughts Regarding Situations You Fear

Situations I Fear	What Do I Fear Will Happen in that Situation?
1.	a. _____ What do I fear will happen next? b. _____ And next? c. _____ And next? d. _____ What do I fear will happen in that situation?
2.	a. _____ What do I fear will happen next? b. _____ And next? c. _____ And next? d. _____ What do I fear will happen in that situation?
3.	a. _____ What do I fear will happen next? b. _____ And next? c. _____ And next? d. _____

involved driving, but each was associated with a different sequence of thoughts. When Irene identified her thought sequences for both situations, she was able to see that she was afraid of two things: being alone and stranded and having other people angry with her. She was then able to deal with each situation separately.

Having identified what you think regarding entering the situation, you will notice that you are not really afraid of the situation but of what you will do in that situation. Let's look at an example.

Richard was afraid of going into stores because it meant he would have to go through checkout lines. He believed that something about checkout lines themselves made him anxious. When I asked what he feared about them, however, he responded that he wasn't afraid of checkout lines per se but of fainting while standing in the line. I asked him if he was afraid of fainting at home. He responded that he wasn't. Why was he afraid of fainting in a checkout line? Because everyone would look at him, and he would be embarrassed.

Asking yourself a series of questions such as I asked Richard enables you to identify the real nature of your fear. In Richard's case—as in most cases—all the answers point to a fear of losing control in some way. Your answers will reveal what specifically about your loss of control you fear. The situation evokes fear because you fear losing control in that situation; perhaps you imagine that you have a greater chance of losing control in that situation. Paradoxically, your belief

Table 7.2 Identifying Your Thoughts Regarding Situations You Fear

	Sample Sheet
Situations I Fear	**What Do I Fear Will Happen in that Situation?**
1. Driving on the interstate	a. *I will have a panic attack.* What do I fear will happen next? b. *I will have to pull off the road.* And next? c. *I will be unable to get going again.* And next? d. *I will be there forever.* What do I fear will happen in that situation?
2. Being stopped at a stoplight during rush hour	a. *I will have a panic attack.* What do I fear will happen next? b. *I will have to stop driving.* And next? c. *The people behind me will be angry with me.* And next? d. _____

that you are likely to lose control in a particular situation is tied to your concerns about what will happen in that situation if you do lose control. One example of this is diagramed in Figure 7.1. The steps are placed in reverse order to illustrate that the expressed fear, really the last to develop, is the first fear that you identify. Ultimately, you are afraid of losing control and embarrassing yourself in public. Fainting is one manifestation of such a loss of control. A checkout line is merely a place where you are likely to lose control in this particular way.

As with symptoms and thoughts, you need to distinguish between the situations and your thoughts. Remember that restaurants, checkout lines, driving, shopping malls, and the like don't cause panic. They are simply settings in which you anticipate and fear behaving inappropriately.

Eliminating Catastrophic Thoughts

Once you have clearly identified what catastrophic thoughts you have during panic attacks, you can develop strategies to cope with these thoughts. Unlike symptom clusters, thought clusters respond to no specific coping strategies; rather, the more cognitive coping strategies in your repertoire, and the better developed they are, the more successful you will be in eliminating catastrophic thoughts. Let's look at some specific strategies and how to use them.

Consulting Health Professionals

Almost every panic attack sufferer I have seen has consulted at least one physician, and more usually consulted several, to learn what is happening to them. When I ask them what they were told, they typically recount a reasonable appraisal of their problems. But, almost always, they have not been reassured by this information. Is this a simple case of stubbornness, of wanting to be sick?

Not at all! The most frequent reason that a physician's reassurances fail to reassure is that the patient has not had all of his or her questions answered, usually because he or she has not asked them. Returning from the doctor's office, the patient is swamped with doubt: how can she or he believe the doctor when all of these questions remain unanswered?

Solution? Carefully prepare a list of the evidence you have for believing you are ill or insane. Write down your evidence and whatever questions you have about it and the condition you fear. You'll use this information to address all of your concerns when you visit your physician. Prepare your physician in advance for what you want to do: make

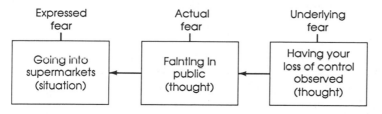

Figure 7.1 Cognitive links in a chain of fear

sure that he or she knows that you wish to discuss these concerns so that you can be scheduled for enough time to do so. Stay until all of your questions are answered; take notes on the answers so that you can remind yourself of them at a later date.

You now have a document that lists both your questions and the evidence that clarifies the answers. Allow yourself the satisfaction of knowing you have coped well with your information vacuum.

Calming Self-Talk

Calming self-talk refers to talking to yourself to reassure yourself both during a panic attack and when anticipating a panic attack. But how do you reassure yourself when all of your thoughts are telling you that you're in grave danger? The hardest time to try to respond calmly to catastrophic thoughts is when you're having a panic attack. Accordingly, you must prepare calming, reassuring responses to such thoughts so that you have them ready to be called upon when you need them. You must go through several steps to do this:

1. Articulate responses to your catastrophic thoughts. These responses should feel genuine to you. You won't be able to fake yourself out with a pep talk while you're having a panic attack.
2. Write your responses down. As you think of catastrophic rejoinders to these responses, you will have to respond to them as well.
3. Rehearse your responses throughout the day or whenever you find yourself beginning to anticipate a panic attack. The more you rehearse and the more convincing your responses are, the more successful you will be at countering catastrophic thoughts.

Checking with a medical specialist beforehand to lay to rest any concerns you may have regarding your physical and mental health also helps you believe your own reassurances.

Calming self-talk is possible even with nightime panic attacks that wake you from deep sleep. In such a case, recall whatever thoughts about your attacks occur to you in the middle of the night and articulate responses to those thoughts. Then you can practice calming yourself down by planning what to do when you wake up in the night having an attack.

Mentally and physically rehearsing how you will deal with a panic attack once it occurs is a powerful tool for coping with the problem for several reasons. First, when rehearsing, *you are in control*: you choose when and how to respond to your thoughts. In the process, you learn to allow negative thoughts to enter your mind, respond to them with calming self-talk, and dismiss the negative thoughts from conscious consideration. Second, in choosing the time and place to address your cognitive fears, you reduce the anxiety associated with the thoughts. By repeatedly recalling your catastrophic thoughts without anxiety in the process of rehearsing, you are, in effect, engaging in a relearning process. Third, you are replacing your catastrophic thoughts with a new, rational set of thoughts that you will then remember when you next encounter panic.

Challenging Your Assumptions

Individuals with panic disorder jump to conclusions about what will happen to them if they feel panic symptoms and how people around them will respond. These conclusions are almost always worst-case scenarios:

- If people see me choke, they will laugh at me.
- If I have to pull off the road, I'll be stuck there forever.
- If I have a panic attack while I'm driving, I'll lose control and kill someone.
- If a panic attack starts, it will never end.

Let's see how you could challenge each of these assumptions.

Assumption	**Challenge**
1. If I choke, people will laugh at me.	Have I ever seen people laugh at someone who was choking? Of course not. If I choke, what people will probably do is try to help me.
2. If I have to pull off the road, I'll be there forever.	Of course I wouldn't be there forever. Either my panic attack would subside and I'd drive off, or someone would come to help me. Panic attacks always end, so I'd be able to drive away. And the police always stop to help cars stopped alongside the road.

3. If I have a panic attack while I'm driving, I'll lose control and kill someone.

I've had panic attacks driving. I've always had enough presence of mind to act appropriately. If my attack really gets worse than it's ever been, I'd have enough warning to take action.

4. If a panic attack starts, it will never end.

Panic attacks always end. That's my experience and the experience of everyone else! There are many things that can be done to terminate a panic attack, and I know many techniques for doing so.

Assessing the Likelihood of Events

Another kind of challenge deserves special attention—challenging your belief that what you fear may happen is likely to happen. What kind of thinking transforms an unlikely event into a likely one? The case of Robert is a good illustration.

Robert was a nonsmoking, healthy 29-year-old who exercised frequently. He had normal blood pressure and no family history of heart disease. His risk of having a heart attack in the next year was extremely low, so low, in fact, that life insurance companies would have eagerly signed him up. But Robert had a panic attack during which his heartbeat was very pronounced, he had chest pain, and his right hand became numb. During this episode, he became acutely afraid that he was having a heart attack. A stress electrocardiogram and ambulatory heart monitor turned up no heart problems. This information calmed Robert's fears for the most part, and he was able to reevaluate his irrational prediction more realistically. Robert had made certain that his physician answered his questions regarding his specific level of risk for heart attacks.

Robert had thought the possibility of having a heart attack during a panic attack was highly likely. Why? The anxiety he felt during his first attack precluded rational assessment of the symptoms he was feeling. Subsequently, with new information, Robert was able to reassess the likelihood of a heart attack more realistically. Making such a realistic assessment is an important first step in estimating the feared outcome of the panic attack.

The truth is that Robert *could* have a heart attack! The truth also is that the likelihood is so low that for him to worry about it is simply irrational.

Once you decide that the likelihood of a feared event is low, write down your realistic assessment and refer to it when in crisis. This information will remind you to appraise the situation realistically. When you, as Robert did, become more realistic in your appraisal, remind yourself frequently of the actual likelihood that your worst-case scenario will play itself out. When a panic attack does come, your rehearsal will allow you to remember the more realistic probability—a probability that you determined while you were thinking rationally.

Paradoxical Intention

Another effective technique for eliminating catastrophic thoughts is called *paradoxical intention*. It is based on the observation that if you set out to produce or allow that which you fear, paradoxically your fear will disappear. Experiencing the feared behavior or thoughts allows you to realize that neither the behavior nor the thought is terrible. Further, by deciding to think the feared thought, you are controlling it rather than it controlling you. Finally, in deciding to think the catastrophic thought, you eliminate the anxiety associated with controlling the thought.

A case of anxiety associated with sexual performance provides an excellent example of how paradoxical intention works. After several attempts at sexual intercourse, a client—Sid—was no longer able to experience an erection long enough to commence intercourse. Humiliated, he steadfastly avoided sexual situations where he might fail at having intercourse. Of course, Sid's original problem, which might have proved transient, was then compounded by his performance anxiety, the combination of which resulted in a permanent problem.

Using paradoxical intention to treat Sid's problem involved prescribing his chief symptom—that is, prescribing a flaccid penis. No longer anxious that he would not have an erection, Sid was then instructed to engage in sex play but not to have intercourse. With the anxiety associated with the pressure to have intercourse removed, Sid was able to enjoy the sex play, become sexually aroused and, in defiance of the therapist's instructions, engage in intercourse.

How would paradox work with the catastrophic thoughts that accompany your panic attacks? One example of this was provided by a colleague who was treating a woman who had panic attacks in shopping centers. During an attack, she would run out of the center, and she subsequently began avoiding shopping centers. An analysis of her thoughts revealed that she was afraid of fainting, and underlying that fear was another fear—that she would be laughed at if she were to faint. The therapist offered this woman the following paradoxical instructions: "Enter a shopping center. Pick a convenient spot and lie down on the floor as if you fainted. Then see what happens. If people come by and ask, tell them you fainted but that you're all right." Her therapist also offered the following rationale: "You are afraid to have a panic attack in which you feel dizzy, because of the possibility of fainting. You are further afraid of being ridiculed should anyone witness you fainting. If you allow yourself to conduct the faked-fainting experiment, you will discover whether or not you have anything to fear." The woman agreed to the experiment and discovered that she was not ridiculed—that, rather, people showed genuine concern. As a consequence, her fear of having an attack diminished greatly, and she again began frequenting shopping centers.

Other examples are easy to find.

- A woman who felt trapped in a classroom during panic attacks mistakenly believed that if she left everyone would stare at her. She was instructed to leave the classroom when she was not having an attack—for practice.
- A man afraid of feeling anxious while driving thought that he would crash his car during an anxiety attack. He was instructed to bring on anxiety while driving to get practice in bringing it under control.
- A woman afraid of having an attack while alone at home feared that she would be unable to obtain emergency help if she needed it. She was told to bring on attacks while at home alone, using hyperventilation, to see what would happen.

The paradoxical technique can easily be adapted to counter your own cognitions and fears. If, for example, you think, "I'm afraid to think of having a panic attack because I'm afraid I'll have one," try it: think about having a panic attack and see if you get one. If you don't, fine; if you do, it will be a wonderful opportunity to practice some of your newly learned coping skills.

With paradoxical techniques, you can't lose. If what you fear will happen doesn't happen, you win because you learn your fear was unfounded. If what you fear will happen does happen, you win because you learn that it's not as terrible as you think, and you get practice at coping with it. The very fact that you're in control because you're allowing what you fear to happen greatly diminishes the anxiety you would normally feel in such a circumstance.

Paradoxical techniques allow you to gain control of your catastrophic thoughts. Remember that these thoughts occur automatically in response to anxiety symptoms and generate additional anxiety. These two negative features—occurring outside of your control and generating additional anxiety—are both eliminated when you decide what thoughts to practice and when. Using paradox is a counterintuitive but effective way to eliminate catastrophic thoughts.

Learning to Recognize Your Coping Skills

I am constantly amazed when talking to panic sufferers to hear them lament their inability to cope with panic attacks when, in fact, they have already developed effective coping strategies. A recent conversation with one such person went something like this:

Roger: During panic attacks, I'm totally unable to think. If I'm reading or studying, I won't even know what I'm reading or studying.

Me: What are you doing when you're unable to concentrate or remember what you're reading?

Roger: I catch myself worrying about things that don't make any sense or that I've thought of ten thousand times before.

Me: What do you do then?

Roger: I take a Xanax, or I stop what I'm doing, take a little break, and talk to myself.

Me: Does it work? Does taking a break and talking to yourself stop your rumination and short-circuit your panic attack?

Roger: Yes, usually.

Me: So . . . you already have an effective strategy for coping with this problem.

Roger: I guess I do.

Me: Why don't you use it all the time? In fact, why don't you plan on using it *before* you study, since you can predict that you're likely to have this problem when you study.

Roger: I think I will.

Roger had a very effective strategy for coping with his preattack anxiety, but he had not been fully aware of his use of this coping strategy and he had not applied it systematically.

You undoubtedly also possess a variety of coping strategies that work. Assessing your coping strategies in Chapter 5 showed you which ones you use and how effective they are. When you sharpen your awareness of the strategies you already use and the success you have already experienced, you will boost your self-efficacy—your knowledge that you can—and to some extent already have—handle any eventuality.

You're Not Dead or Crazy Yet!

Are you? Of course not, or you wouldn't be reading this. But does one of your catastrophic thoughts express the fear that your attacks will lead to death or insanity? How long have you had panic attacks? Are you dead? Are you crazy? If not, you must be doing something right. You must, in fact, be coping with your attacks. Your attacks always end, don't they? If you think about it carefully, you can probably identify what you do that helps some attacks be less severe and shorter in duration. The problem is that you have trouble connecting your efforts with the end of a panic attack. Part of the problem is recognizing your effort. Only then can you be clear about its effect on your attacks.

Panic attacks do not lead to death.

Likewise, panic attacks do not lead to going crazy.

The truth is they are extremely uncomfortable. By their nature they induce fears of some ultimate disaster. What they don't induce is the ultimate disaster itself. When you analyze your own experiences in the light of these facts, you will have another piece of evidence that your attacks are something you yourself can master.

Summary

In this chapter you've learned to cope with the catastrophic thoughts that accompany and follow panic attacks. You've learned to:

1. Differentiate your thoughts from your symptoms.
2. Differentiate your thoughts from situations in which attacks occur.
3. Talk to professionals to obtain the facts you need to know about your own level of risk.
4. Practice calming self-talk as a way of dealing with catastrophic thoughts.
5. Examine and challenge your assumptions about what will happen if you have a panic attack.
6. Realistically assess the probability of feared events and remind yourself of this assessment in situations where you can expect to be panicky.
7. Use paradoxical intention to learn the truth about your false beliefs.
8. Realize that you have been using coping techniques all along to reduce and control your panic attacks.

After all, you're not dead or crazy yet!

8

Strategies in Action

*H*aving learned various strategies for coping with panic symptoms and catastrophic cognitions, you are ready to consider some further refinements in applying them. In this chapter, we will look at how to match specific coping strategies with specific symptoms. Then we will examine some guidelines for sequencing strategies during a panic attack and for the events that precede an attack. Finally, we will explore ways in which you can field-test your coping strategies, an approach roughly analogous to testing a new weapons system in the "real" world of simulated war.

Matching Coping Strategies to Symptoms

Though the coping strategies discussed in the previous chapters have been used to relieve all the symptoms of panic, my research and clinical observations have demonstrated the wisdom of matching strategies to symptoms. Let me first remind you of the principal types of symptoms of panic attacks:

1. feelings of disorientation
2. general autonomic arousal
3. stomach distress
4. numbness or tingling
5. chest discomfort
6. nausea

We will also be considering several other panic symptoms that do not fall into easily classified groups:

1. difficulty swallowing
2. cold hands and feet
3. sensitivity to noise
4. blurred vision

Table 8.1 shows the coping strategies recommended for each of these symptom groups. As you can see, diaphragmatic breathing is useful in reducing each of the six main symptom groups. This is not to say that it will always prove effective, only that it is a generally useful strategy in coping with all types of symptoms.

Many techniques are useful for alleviating disorientation, and physical distraction can be especially effective in dealing with the mental confusion and dizziness that characterize disorientation. Such distractions as hobbies, housework, and taking a shower shift your focus from within to without, particularly useful because disorientation is such an intensely personal experience. Calming self-talk and general relaxation are also effective for reducing feelings of disorientation.

Table 8.1 Coping Strategies Tailored to Specific Symptoms

Symptoms	*Coping Strategies to Use*
Disorientation	
Feeling unreal	Relaxation exercise
Dizzy	Diaphragmatic breathing
Disconnected from body	Physical distraction
Confused	Mental distraction
	Self-talk
Chest discomfort	
Heart beats rapidly	Relaxation exercise
Heart pounding	Diaphragmatic breathing
Feeling of suffocation	Mental distraction
Shortness of breath	Self-talk
Stomach distress	Diaphragmatic breathing
Numbness or tingling in body	Mental distraction
	Diaphragmatic breathing
	Self-talk
Nausea	Mental distraction
	Diaphragmatic breathing
	Self-talk
Difficulty swallowing	Physical distraction
	Relaxation exercise
Cold hands or feet	Physical distraction
	Relaxation exercise
Sensitivity to noise	Passive distraction
Blurred vision	Passive distraction

Chest discomfort, too, responds well to a number of coping strategies. Direct interventions such as relaxation exercises and diaphragmatic breathing coupled with calming self-talk are effective. Indirect strategies such as mental distraction shift your attention away from the symptoms.

Stomach distress, on the other hand, has very few coping strategies associated with it. Only diaphragmatic breathing has been found to be useful.

Nausea and numbness or tingling in your body can both be countered with mental distraction and calming self-talk in addition to controlled breathing. Such symptoms apparently produce panic cognitions that in turn exacerbate the symptoms if not combated with self-talk and mental distraction.

Relaxation exercises and physical distraction can be used to cope effectively with difficulty swallowing and cold hands and feet. These relatively mild symptoms typically do not trigger catastrophic cognitions and hence do not require self-talk.

Sensitivity to noise and blurred vision both respond best to passive distraction strategies such as talking to someone, lying down, watching television, and reading. These symptoms may be more closely related to external stress and therefore respond best to a reduction in stress.

Coping Strategies and Catastrophic Cognitions

You will notice that I do not recommend specific coping strategies for specific catastrophic cognitions. I did not find evidence in either my research or clinical experience to indicate that any specific coping strategy is effective with any specific cognitions. Select your own strategies for dealing with your thoughts, based on personal preference and trial and error.

Sequencing Your Strategies

As I stated earlier, the more coping strategies you have at your disposal, the more likely you will be to overcome your panic attacks. Having a number of strategies in your coping repertoire will give you greater flexibility and a stronger sense of self-efficacy as you systematically attack your panic. As you test your strategies to see what works best, you will discard some and fine-tune others. This is a natural process as you learn to cope with panic. For any single panic attack correct sequencing of your coping strategies increases the chance of quickly bringing the attack under control. Here are some broad guidelines for establishing a sequence for these strategies that will let you obtain the maximum benefit from them.

Step 1: Gather Information

The first step, and, therefore, in many ways, the most important, is to use strategies that yield information. It is imperative that you:

1. Take stock of *what* is happening to you.
2. Determine *why* it is happening now.
3. Distinguish what you are *feeling* from what you are *thinking*.

If you have this information, your panic attack is much less likely to worsen, because accurate information about what is happening will short-circuit the catastrophic cognitions that escalate attacks. Knowing what is going on and why it is going on means your catastrophic thoughts aren't being fueled. Having taken stock of your symptoms and thoughts, you can make informed decisions about which coping strategies are most likely to help you.

Step 2: Take Aim at Your Thoughts

Because your thoughts about what is happening during a panic attack are so important to its progression, your second tactic should be to target the catastrophic cognitions that follow the sudden onset of symptoms. Your first aim should be to reduce the severity of your attacks, a goal best accomplished by changing your thoughts. So, postpone dealing with your symptoms now and concentrate on your cognitions. What cognitive strategies should you use and in what order? You used one cognitive strategy in the first step when you distinguished what you were feeling from what you were thinking. Challenging those thoughts directly by assessing the probability of disastrous events, scanning your memory for facts you've learned about your attacks, and calming yourself down with a realistic appraisal of the situation are all effective ways to deal with thoughts on the verge of being out of control. There is no persuasive argument for choosing one of these first and another second. Your choice should be based on which strategy appeals most to you or seems easiest to implement during an actual attack.

Step 3: Take Aim at Your Symptoms

Once your thoughts are under control, you can deal more effectively with your symptoms. You will find that as you repeatedly practice your strategies in the actual circumstance of a panic attack, your thoughts will lose much of their power. This will leave room (and energy!) to cope effectively with your symptoms.

You must know what your body is feeling before you can choose appropriate coping strategies. So take the time to discover this, making certain that you are separating your symptoms from your thoughts. Select coping strategies that you think will be effective in relieving your symptoms and then decide which strategies to use first and which to use later on. You'll be selecting from two different kinds of strategies: direct and indirect.

Direct strategies are those that focus squarely on the symptoms; examples include relaxation, diaphragmatic breathing, and calming self-talk. Diaphragmatic breathing can, in itself, for example, directly alleviate the feeling of suffocation experienced by many panic sufferers. Indirect strategies, on the other hand, are sensory, physical, and mental distractions that alleviate a symptom by shifting the focus of attention away from the symptom.

Choose direct strategies that require little effort over more indirect strategies. Direct strategies increase your self-efficacy more than indirect strategies do and are more easily applied. Indirect strategies require more effort to implement: going outside to walk in the snow requires more effort than telling yourself to relax, for instance. And since indirect strategies don't reduce symptoms through an easily identifiable cause-and-effect action, you are less likely to recognize such strategies as controlling your symptoms.

Step 4: Allow an Attack to Happen

Although rare, sometimes even after you have used all your strategies, your panic attack will continue. When this happens, you must be prepared to ride out the attack. If your attacks tend to last longer than an hour, accepting the attack is often useful even while you are applying other strategies. Distraction techniques, for example, generally do not eliminate panic symptoms. The continuance of the attack at a lesser level therefore doesn't mean your strategies aren't working. It does mean that you will have to stop struggling against your symptoms and accept them, even as you use the strategies at your disposal.

Field-Testing Your Strategies

Developing faith in your ability to deal effectively with panic attacks— self-efficacy—is a function of several different factors. The principal factor affecting self-efficacy is the feedback you receive from taking action. If you actively cope with your panic, you will rapidly come to believe in your ability to do so. In other words, your thoughts follow your actions—belief in yourself follows acting efficaciously.

Is this cause and effect the reverse of what you expect? You probably assume that your thoughts precede your actions. You may think that your actions follow a decision to do something. In this line of thinking, to deal with panic attacks, you would have to believe in your ability to cope *before* you put yourself in a situation where you would have to cope.

But what actually happens is a more complex interaction between your beliefs and your actions. Imagine that you decided to learn a new skill—diving. The process wouldn't consist of deciding to dive and then diving, period. It would be much more interactive. After you decided to learn to dive, you would rehearse mentally how you would do it. This mental rehearsal would culminate in an actual attempt to dive, in which your body would try to reproduce what you had rehearsed mentally. The feedback from your dive would provide you with more information. If your dive was effective, you would have entered the water cleanly and painlessly. If less effective, some negative feedback, perhaps in the form of pain, would indicate that. Further mental and actual rehearsal, additional decisions, and repeated feedback would gradually shape your dive into a thing of beauty.

Learning to cope with panic attacks is similar. Having read about strategies for coping with both panic symptoms and catastrophic cognitions, you have in effect begun to form mental images of how to implement these strategies. The actual translation of these strategies into action is the process by which your brain and body transform this information into knowledge, a process we discussed earlier. Practicing strategies for coping with panic when you are feeling no significant amount of anxiety is akin to practicing diving in your living room. Such practice is an important step in the learning process. You are developing skills that you will later transfer to the actual situation.

To ensure that these skills will transfer to an actual panic attack and that they will be effective, you can apply three techniques:

1. *Imaginal practice:* Induce panic symptoms and the thoughts that go with them by imagining a panic attack. The more closely the situation you imagine resembles an actual situation in which you panic, the more effectively you will be able to use your coping strategies in that situation.
2. *Prepanic preparation:* Rehearse your techniques before you enter situations that you expect will trigger panic. This preparation will make a panic attack less likely while increasing the likelihood that you will successfully cope with an attack should it occur.
3. *Conducting a trial run:* Induce panic symptoms and thoughts in actual situations in which you fear a panic attack will occur. Dealing effectively with them will further increase your self-

efficacy and improve your ability to cope with panic in any circumstance. Let's look at how to implement each of these techniques.

Imaginal Practice

Whenever you let your imagination dwell on the circumstances of your panic attacks—whether that be the symptoms, thoughts, or situation— a strange thing happens: you begin to experience the symptoms of an attack. Though uncomfortable, you can use this phenomenon to retrain your body and mind to cope effectively with your symptoms. Such retraining is based on state-dependent learning, a phenomenon in which your recall improves when your mental and emotional states resemble those under which you learned a behavior. If you learn to cope with your panic symptoms and thoughts under conditions that approximate panic attacks, you will be better able to remember those coping strategies in an actual panic attack.

Imaginal practice is one way to practice coping strategies under conditions similar *but not identical* to panic attacks. The symptoms and thoughts you experience in imagining an attack will be similar to but less severe than those you have during panic. Thus, you can simulate the panic without having to endure its full force and, in the process, learn how to cope with your actual feelings.

The procedure you use in imaginal practice is fairly straightforward:

1. Find a quiet and comfortable place to practice.
2. Recall the coping strategies that you have chosen to help you deal with both your symptoms and your thoughts. Writing them down in the order in which you plan to use them is helpful.
3. Recall your most recent panic attack.
4. Begin at a point before the attack actually began. Remember where you were and what you were doing. Proceed in your imagination to the point at which you began to experience the panic attack.
5. Identify the specific symptoms you felt at the beginning of the attack. You will immediately notice the intrusion of a number of thoughts following the symptoms.
6. Differentiate the symptoms from the thoughts.
7. Institute the strategy or strategies you have chosen to cope with your cognitions. I recommend that you deal with your cognitions before dealing with your symptoms because your cognitions, if unchecked, will escalate your attack and interfere with your ability to cope with your symptoms. Once you have dealt with your catastrophic cognitions, you can then direct your attention to reducing your symptoms.

8. Replay the entire scenario again, going slowly so that you clearly identify your symptoms and thoughts and experience the effect of your coping strategies on both.
9. Continue to repeat the scene until you begin to develop a sense of mastery over both your thoughts and symptoms.

Your first attempts at using imagery to induce a semblance of panic will likely prove difficult since your experience will be similar to that of an actual attack. You need to remember that this is to be expected and is precisely what you need to gain confidence in your ability to cope with the panic attacks themselves.

As you practice coping with your induced panic symptoms, you will notice that some strategies work better than others. Discard the strategies that don't work for you and continue to develop those that do work. One of the aims of your field-testing is to identify what strategies work best for you.

Imaginal practice is a skill that, like any skill, improves with practice. Practice coping with your panic attacks imaginally at least several times a week, or, if possible, daily. Set aside ample time—an hour or more—to practice. You need this time to incorporate the necessary details into your imaginal practice. An hour or more will also allow you to repeat the entire scene at least once—and preferably twice—so that you begin to experience mastery over the situation.

Prepanic Preparation: A Preventative

Though panic attacks sometimes occur spontaneously, they often occur in identifiable situations. Because you learn to associate these specific situations with panic, you experience anticipatory anxiety when entering them. Sometimes you actually avoid situations in which you anticipate panicking. The subject of avoidance and what to do about it is examined in Chapters 9 and 10. Right now, we are concerned with situations that you don't avoid but in which you expect you might have a panic attack.

Preparing for panic—which translates into figuring out in advance what you will do should you have either a partial or full-fledged panic attack—is an extremely effective way to prevent attacks. Notice that I said *prevent* attacks, not cope with them or reduce their severity. Preparing to cope with an attack helps ensure that an attack will not happen.

A subtle factor is operating here. If you hope against hope that a panic attack won't occur, you will be unable to prepare yourself for one. Preparing yourself admits of the possibility that you will have an attack. The combination of accepting this possibility and planning your strategy will help prevent an attack from happening.

How do you prepare for an attack? The procedure is similar to that outlined in the previous section on imaginal practice. Rather than focusing on your most recent attack, however, you project into the future to develop your strategy. Two examples will illustrate the procedure.

Example 1. Robert was afraid to drive, yet drove 35 miles for our appointments, always, however, accompanied by his daughter. We were working toward his driving alone to the next appointment. He informed me that driving alone to the appointment would be no problem; I would be waiting, and he would be driving to a safe harbor. It was in driving home that he anticipated and feared having a panic attack. Robert identified several features of the drive home that heightened his sense of anticipation:

1. There would be no one waiting for him at home.
2. He would have to drive home in the dark, whereas he would be driving to our appointment during the day.
3. He would have to cross a bridge on the way home, a challenge complicated by its being dark.

These situations were a problem not in themselves but because of what they meant if he had a panic attack:

1. No one would miss his not coming home; therefore, he would be stranded forever.
2. In the dark, no one would notice that his car was pulled over while he was having a panic attack.
3. He would be unable to pull over on the bridge should an attack strike while he was crossing the bridge.

I persuaded him to come alone to the next session. In that session, we worked on thinking through his responses to these possibilities, and he developed the following strategies:

1. He would let his daughter know that he would call her when he got home and what time she should expect his call.
2. He would turn on his emergency flashers to let someone know he was in distress if waiting out his attack did not allow him to continue home.
3. If he panicked on the bridge, he would handle his panic attack using deep breathing until he arrived at the other side of the bridge. Then he would pull over if he needed to until his panic attack was under control.

He rehearsed these strategies in his imagination several times before he left the session. He then drove home knowing what he would do if he had a panic attack. No such attack occurred, however; he had successfully prevented one through careful strategic planning.

Example 2. Judith was afraid of having a panic attack in the dentist's chair. She had continued to visit her dentist regularly but always felt anxious while going and while there. Her principal fear was that she would have a panic attack while the dentist was working on her teeth and would jump up and run out of his office during a procedure.

Together we planned the following strategy, which she then practiced in imagination. We first determined that though her panic would escalate if she were unable to "escape" while her teeth were being worked on, it would be relatively manageable in the early phases. When she followed her thoughts, she discovered that her underlying fear was of leaping from the chair and embarrassing herself. To cope, Judith needed to feel more in control. She decided that if she were able to signal her dentist that she needed him to stop working so she could sit up or stretch for a minute, then she would feel more in control of the situation. She decided that she would use a hand signal for this purpose and, further, that she would discuss such a signal with her dentist before she came for her appointment. Her dentist thought the idea a good one, since he had seen her highly anxious at other times.

Because she now felt in control, Judith experienced no panic and, in fact, much less anxiety during her next visit to the dentist. Again, working out a coping strategy *in case* she had a panic attack prevented an attack.

Both Robert and Judith anticipated having panic attacks and felt a great deal of anxiety before they even entered the situations they feared. Because they anticipated their attacks, they could work out coping strategies in advance. Doing this in imaginal practice increased their sense of being able to cope and, further, permitted them to examine their anticipated fears and solutions in detail.

Imaginal practice and prepanic preparation can both be adapted to your individual problems. Remember, imaginal practice enables you to identify your symptoms and thoughts. Then, after carefully choosing appropriate coping strategies, you can practice handling them.

Conducting a Trial Run

Though both imaginal practice and prepanic preparation are usually sufficient to produce the desired effect—self-efficacy regarding your ability to deal with panic, its precursors, and its consequences— sometimes an additional step must be taken. This step is reserved for those who, in spite of success in dealing with panic symptoms and cognitions in imagery, have failed to develop a complete sense of self-efficacy in coping with "real" panic. They persist in dreading panic attacks, believing that they will be unable to cope with them should they occur.

In such cases, the panic sufferer should purposefully induce panic symptoms, using either imagery techniques or hyperventilation, in an actual situation in which he or she has panicked in the past.

Annie, who was terrified of having a panic attack while her husband was out of town and she was home alone, developed the following treatment program:

1. She developed coping skills using imagery until she felt confident in these skills. She practiced these techniques first while her husband was at home and then while he was at work.

2. She practiced inducing panic symptoms through hyperventilation and then gaining control of these symptoms, first while her husband was at home and then while he was at work.

3. She induced both her panic symptoms and her preprogrammed catastrophic thoughts and then coped with both of these. Again, she did this first while her husband was at home and then while he was at work. At this point she felt considerable self-efficacy but still doubted her ability to deal with a panic attack alone while her husband was out of town.

4. The next stage of treatment, therefore, consisted of prepanic preparation during a period just before her husband was to leave on a business trip. In this phase, she utilized fantasy both to induce panic symptoms and to imagine how she would cope with them. In her fantasy, she imagined being alone without her husband to assist her. She then imagined having a panic attack, complete with catastrophic thoughts, and using her coping skills to gain control of both the thoughts and the symptoms.

5. Annie's final step was to induce her panic symptoms and catastrophic thoughts while her husband was out of town. Although she was afraid, Annie was able to cope effectively with her symptoms and thoughts. The experience solidified her confidence in her ability to deal with any eventuality.

Annie's treatment program was thoroughly mapped out: you can see the steady progression of treatment and how one success experience prepared her for the next. Keep in mind that the goal of this type of treatment is not to convince yourself that you will never have another panic attack but that you can deal with them if and when they do recur.

Reducing Your Vulnerability to Panic— Dealing with Precursors

We have seen how panic attacks grow out of a heightened level of general anxiety caused by chronic conflict and life stressors. Because the panic attacks themselves are so powerful, reducing them is your first priority, and the procedures for sequencing and field-testing coping strategies will guide you through this process. Once you begin to feel in control of the attacks themselves, you should focus your attention on the elements that led to their development, the precursors to your attacks.

Interpersonal problems and other sources of conflict and stress are often precursors to panic. Accordingly, resolving these problems can help reduce or eliminate panic attacks. Resolving the cause, you resolve the consequence, except in those instances where the panic attacks have become autonomous. Depending on your appraisal of the cause of your attacks, you can take one of three approaches to coping with precursors:

1. Remove the problem. Taking this approach presumes that the problem can be resolved directly. Examples include resolving a conflicted marriage through divorce, a horrible job by getting a transfer, or a belief you have AIDS by getting a blood test to determine whether or not you have antibodies for the AIDS virus. As is clear from these examples, many times, resolving a problem directly can be difficult or impossible.

2. Accept the problem and accommodate to it. If you choose not to end an unhappy marriage, accept the limits of the relationship, do what you can to improve it within those limits, and seek satisfaction in other pursuits. If you have a chronic physical illness, accept it and figure out your life options. A star football player who found himself a paraplegic as the result of an accident, for example, went on a lecture circuit to inform high school students of the dangers of driving while drinking.

3. Accept the problem and cope directly with its consequences, including any depression, anxiety, and physical or mental illness. Cope with your depression following the death of your spouse by dealing consciously with your negative thoughts, for example. Cope with panic triggered by an unresolvable conflict by learning to reduce the symptoms and thoughts that accompany it.

Since panic attacks often follow a fluctuating course—disappearing for a time and then reappearing—they quite possibly may follow the course of the problems that led to them. When these problems are resolved either totally or partially, permanently or temporarily, the panic attacks subside. When the problems recur, the panic attacks likewise return. If this pattern characterizes your attacks, you must resolve the recurring conflict or stress if you want to end your panic attacks permanently.

Summary

In this chapter, we have focused on the steps involved in putting coping strategies in action. Let's review what we have learned:

1. Certain strategies are particularly effective in coping with specific symptom clusters.
2. No specific strategies have been found to counter specific catastrophic thoughts.
3. We examined four guidelines to follow in establishing a sequence for the coping strategies you have chosen: (a) gather information, (b) take aim at your thoughts, (c) take aim at your symptoms, and (d) allow an attack to happen.
4. To move toward eliminating your panic attacks, once you have learned, selected, and sequenced your basic coping strategies, you must try them out in ever more realistic situations, a process called field-testing your strategies.
5. Field-testing can be accomplished in three ways: (a) through imaginal practice, (b) through prepanic preparation, and (c) through conducting a trial run in an actual situation in which you fear panicking. People seldom need to use all three procedures to eliminate their attacks; usually, using the first or first and second suffices.
6. After reducing the frequency and severity of your panic attacks, you must deal with the precursors of panic—the anxiety, conflicts, and stress that lead to your attacks—if you want to end your attacks permanently.
7. You can choose among three basic approaches to dealing with precursors: (a) remove the problem, (b) accept the problem and accommodate to it, and (c) accept the problem and cope directly with its consequences.

9

The What and Why of Avoidance Strategies

*T*his will be the most painful chapter for anyone who uses avoidance strategies to deal with panic—most painful because avoidance strategies work, over the short run, to reduce the anxiety that the panic disorder sufferer anticipates or actually experiences. A strategy that works, even over the short run, is hard to relinquish, and so the panic attack sufferer will battle whomever or whatever he or she must to keep avoiding. In this chapter, we will examine what avoidance strategies are and how they develop. In the next chapter, we will examine counter strategies to aid you in breaking your pattern of avoidance.

What Are Avoidance Strategies?

Simply put, avoidance strategies are attempts to deal with anxiety by staying away from anxiety-provoking situations. Avoidance strategies may be verbal, mental, or behavioral. They also may be obvious or subtle. Consider the following examples:

- not eating in restaurants
- not going to concerts or participating in any activities that involve a crowd, even though you previously enjoyed these activities
- driving 50 miles farther to avoid driving on an interstate highway
- not talking about the situations you avoid
- providing good reasons for avoiding a situation you fear
- accusing anyone who tries to get you to confront a situation you fear of not understanding your problem
- verbally attacking anyone who tries to get you to confront your avoidance, thus diverting attention from your avoidance to your verbal attack
- getting friends or family members to accompany you without telling them why

- attributing successful confrontation of a situation you fear to someone who has told you to confront it (you could not do it on your own)
- driving thoughts of what you fear and how you might cope with it out of your mind
- confronting a situation you fear only at special times so that you can deny your ability to confront it at any other time.
- denying successful confrontations by attributing them to necessity, luck, or other external circumstances

You can see from the above examples that there are basically three types of avoidance: (1) not entering situations you normally enter or previously entered, (2) using verbal tactics to divert your and other people's attention from the fact that you avoid certain situations, and (3) thinking about the situations you fear and the ways in which you confront them in such a way that you *believe* you are avoiding those situations.

This last type of avoidance requires some additional explanation, since it does not appear to fit the definition of avoidance I gave earlier. I have included it because your own perception of whether or not you are avoiding situations is critical. If you confront a situation *only because you were told to*, your perception will be that you continue to avoid it. Only when you perceive your confrontation as under your control will you consider it nonavoidance.

Escape strategies are often more automatic than avoidance strategies. Escape is the strategy you use when, anticipating or experiencing a panic attack, you leave the situation you are in. Escape strategies are related to avoidance strategies in that you are more likely to avoid a situation if you have a history of escaping from that situation. If, for example, you leave a party because of a panic attack, you are more likely to decline future invitations to parties.

How Do Avoidance Strategies Develop?

Several principles underlie the development of avoidance strategies in dealing with panic attacks. We will examine two different examples to illustrate what avoidance is and then examine how attempts to deal with panic attacks may lead to avoidance behavior. Let's begin with Ruth.

Ruth had a panic attack while waiting in a supermarket checkout line. Unable to make sense of what was happening, she connected the grocery shopping with having panic attacks. She then logically concluded that, to avoid panic attacks, she needed to avoid grocery shopping. This wasn't easy to do, though, because, of course, if she didn't buy groceries, her family wouldn't eat. Ruth began to think of herself as "odd—a screwball—looney tunes"—after all, everyone she knew was able to shop. She felt unable to deal with this problem of panic attacks. She continued to grocery shop but altered her shopping habits to accommodate her ideas of what may have caused her attack. Since she felt hot during her attack, she avoided going to the grocery store in the heat of the day. Since it was crowded when she had her first attack, she began to go at odd times, when few other shoppers were out and she could get through the checkout line quickly. Since she had been shopping alone when she panicked, she began to shop with friends or insist that her husband accompany her or do the shopping himself. Most of the time these strategies seemed to work: she had few panic attacks while shopping. It didn't occur to her that, until recently, she had had no attacks—without using any avoidance strategies. Using them led her to increasingly believe that she could not shop without using them.

How did Ruth come to use avoidance strategies?

1. She had a spontaneous panic attack in a grocery store.
2. She connected the panic attack with being in the grocery store, but she needed to continue to get groceries, so . . .
3. She attributed her problem to herself—she was "looney tunes."
4. She hypothesized a connection between specific features of the grocery store and her panic attacks. By avoiding these features, she reasoned, she could continue to shop.
5. She also began using subtle avoidance strategies—that is, strategies unlikely to be detected by anyone but her.
6. She considered her use of these strategies further evidence of her inability to cope effectively with panic attacks.

Ruth's thoughts about how she continued to be able to shop for groceries usually took one of the following forms:

- Sure, I went to the store, but only when it was empty. I couldn't have gone if it were crowded.
- Sure, I went to the store, but only because my husband was with me. I couldn't have gone without him.
- I just had to go to the store. We needed the food, and no one else was around to go.
- I didn't think about it. If I had thought about it, I wouldn't have been able to go.

Ruth met any attempt to show her that she, in fact, regularly confronted the situation she feared with a barrage of details about her fear and explanations of how her confrontation of her fear really wasn't a confrontation at all. Both in perceiving her avoidance as evidence of her inability to handle the stress of grocery shopping and in denying responsibility for any success she had at shopping, Ruth accepted responsibility for her failures but not for her accomplishments.

Let's consider another example. You've never in your life had a panic attack, and you're sitting in a restaurant with three friends from your bridge club, far from the door or the rest room. Suddenly, you begin to feel jittery and hot for no apparent reason. You hope your friends don't notice. Your heart springs to a gallop, and your throat feels as though it's closing up. The thought of taking another bite of your food scares you, because you know you'd choke. You're sure that your friends are wondering what's wrong with you and why you're not eating. You're wondering what's wrong with you. You think of excusing yourself and going to the rest room, but you're convinced that everyone with you—in fact, everyone in the restaurant—will know that something is very wrong with you. Somehow you manage to get through the meal without saying a word about what is going on. What would you have said anyway—that you're falling apart or going crazy? You spend the week dreading a recurrence of your experience and wondering what you can do to make sure it doesn't happen again. You're not quite sure what it is you don't want to happen again—the terrible feelings or being trapped and unable to leave when you're having those feelings. Without thinking it through very much, you excuse yourself from eating with the same group of friends the next week, somehow equating eating in a restaurant with the attack and the subsequent feeling of being trapped. Canceling the luncheon engagement feels bad, since you'll miss the company, and it further convinces you that you couldn't handle such a situation a second time. The fact that you did handle it the first time is not at all obvious.

What is happening? How have you and Ruth ended up developing avoidance strategies and how are they maintained?

Faulty Thinking

Faulty thinking is the basis for avoidance strategies.

Let's examine some of the faulty logic apparent in Ruth's thinking:

Observation: I had that attack when a lot of people were grocery shopping.
Premise: A lot of people must make me nervous.
Conclusion: I'll shop when nobody else is in the store.

Observation: I had the attack when I was shopping alone.
Premise: Shopping alone is risky.
Conclusion: I'll take my husband along and he'll prevent me from having attacks or take care of me if I have an attack.

Premise: Anybody who panics at grocery shopping must be crazy.
Observation: I panicked while grocery shopping.
Conclusion: I must be crazy.

In the imaginary case of you in the restaurant, the following thinking is obvious:

Observation: I had the attack in the restaurant.
Premise: If I go back to the restaurant, I'll have another attack.
Conclusion: I had better avoid the restaurant.

Premise 1: Anybody who feels that way must be crazy.
Premise 2: If I tell my friends how I'm feeling, they'll know I'm crazy.
Conclusion: I can't tell my friends how I'm feeling.

Observation: I felt trapped when I was in the restaurant.
Premise: Being in the restaurant trapped me.
Conclusion: I had better stay out of the restaurant.

Such faulty thinking seems to underlie avoidance as a coping strategy, though it does not actually characterize it. By this I mean that avoiders do not necessarily engage in faulty thinking so explicitly; rather, it is *as if* such logical reasoning were taking place.

"I can't tell my friends how I'm feeling" is the logical conclusion from two faulty premises. But intervening rational thoughts can challenge such conclusions: to assert that the feelings that characterize a panic attack mean that you are crazy is erroneous, as is asserting that your friends will interpret your feelings as crazy. You can therefore change your decision to avoid telling them by challenging your faulty thinking.

When panicking, you are usually overwhelmed with anxiety and thus are not thinking clearly, so you inevitably arrive at faulty conclusions. At the same time, your conclusions seem self-evident; you are so acutely aware of your own thoughts that you believe that everyone will think of your situation the same way you do.

Avoidance behavior naturally follows from these faulty thoughts. "If my friends will think I'm crazy if I tell them what I'm feeling, it makes sense not to tell them. If being in a restaurant caused my attack, it makes sense to stay out of the restaurant." Since little of your thinking during a panic attack is logical, the conclusions you reach and your subsequent avoidance are both natural and predictable consequences.

Action is Information

How you behave during an attack provides you with information on how you handle attacks.

We've seen how actions convey information and how the information bundle associated with a panic attack can lead to further attacks. The same mechanism functions in the development of avoidance behavior. When you experience a highly emotional event, all of the circumstances surrounding the event become bundled in your memory. You remember the environment, your feelings, your thoughts, and your actions. If you find yourself once again in the environment where the event occurred or in similar circumstances, you will automatically recall the details of the event. Less obviously, experiencing the same feelings or feelings similar to those that accompanied the event will also produce a flood of memories of the event.

When depressed for other reasons, for example, you tend to recall events in your life associated with depression. You may remember losing a beloved animal, being humiliated by your peers, or failing in school. Similarly, behavior in which you have engaged at times of stress, when repeated, is capable of eliciting memories and feelings associated with that stress. For example, if you habitually clench your teeth and fists while visiting the dentist, clenching your teeth and fists in other circumstances at a later time may bring to mind the feelings and thoughts you associate with being at the dentist. This means that traumatic events—which, again, are stored in memory as bundles of information including environmental cues, thoughts, feelings, and actions—can be recalled when any one of these four pieces of information is accessed. The question "do we run because we are afraid or are we afraid because we run?" can be answered. It is not that one causes the other, but rather that they are stored together in memory and either will be recalled if triggered by the other.

If, during a panic attack, you avoid the situation you are in or escape from it, this becomes information that your body and mind remembers. The next time you experience panic attack symptoms, you will probably also recall the information that you avoid situations in which you panic.

How does all this affect your future behavior? Essentially, it means that every time you encounter a situation that scares you and you leave it or avoid it, you teach yourself to avoid that situation. Your leaving becomes information to you both about how you deal with severe anxiety and about the severity of your anxiety itself. The same holds true for the opposite response: if you don't leave a situation in which you experience panic, you teach yourself not to leave. The action of leaving or not leaving is information you convey to yourself about your ability to deal with the situation. The equation is simple: if you run from the situation, you tell yourself by your action that you cannot handle the stress; if you stay in the situation, you tell yourself by your action that you can handle the stress, at least to the extent of staying. Paying attention to your success in staying and acknowledging it is also important, of course. Once you begin accumulating information that says you can face a situation that arouses panic, your panic attack itself becomes something that you can handle and don't have to run away from.

Nothing Succeeds Like Success

People continue avoiding and escaping situations they fear because these strategies work.

What is the purpose of avoidance and escape? Simply put, their purpose is to reduce anxiety. And they succeed—both are extremely effective ways of reducing anxiety.

As discussed earlier, escape and avoidance are related but distinct behaviors. Escape is a natural response to a situation appraised as dangerous. This response usually arises during a panic attack or when an attack appears imminent. Avoidance, on the other hand, is a response to anticipatory anxiety, a milder form of anxiety that precedes the acute anxiety you experience during a panic attack. If you have a panic attack while in a store checkout line and consequently leave the store, you are escaping the threat. If you refuse to return to the store to retrieve your purchases because you fear you'll have another panic attack, you are avoiding it.

By leaving and not returning to the store, you reduce your anxiety in two ways. First, you short-circuit the escalation to panic levels of anxiety. Second, returning to the store would put you back in the conflict situation, causing you to again decide between staying or leaving. This conflict would further increase your anxiety. Since you have avoided both sources of anxiety, you feel immediate relief—your anxiety level drops. Because this drop in anxiety is very rewarding, you are likely to repeat this sequence in the future.

Why Do Some People Choose Avoidance Strategies?

We have seen that avoidance strategies develop for three reasons: (1) faulty thinking leads you to conclude that avoidance is the best strategy to follow, (2) your avoidance in itself conveys the information that you cannot cope with the situation you are avoiding, and (3) avoidance works, over the short term, to reduce anxiety. Many people who have anxiety attacks never adopt avoidance strategies, however. Why do some people adopt them and others not? The answer lies in the severity of their panic attacks and in their early learning with regard to stress. Let's examine each of these.

The Severity of the Panic Attack

The more severe your panic attack, the more likely a flight response will *automatically kick in.*

Our early ancestors lived in an environment much more hazardous than ours. Danger, in the form of predatory animals or hostile neighbors, directly threatened our ancestors' very existence. In this environment, those with the most alert senses and responsive nervous systems were most likely to successfully fight or flee their adversaries. The bodily reactions that prepared them for these responses included increased respiration, the pumping of blood to muscles and away from internal organs, and increased muscle contraction—changes identical to those experienced at the beginning of a panic attack. In circumstances of real threat, the response made sense, just as it would today if you walked into a room and were confronted with a tiger. It is easy to understand how maladaptive a rational, well-thought-out analysis would be when facing a tiger; the tiger would leap on you while you were analyzing the data. The bodily responses are the basis for the flight response; the flight response is *built into* the panic reaction.

If the flight response is built into the panic reaction, the more severe your feelings of panic, the more likely you will be to respond automatically by fleeing the situation. Our bodies and brains are wired to insure the greatest chances for survival. The more severe the threat, therefore, the more intense your body's reaction should be, and the greater the likelihood that you will automatically flee. Recent research evidence indicates that this is, in fact, the case: escape behavior related to panic attacks has been shown to be directly related to the severity of the attack.

But if you automatically flee, how can you learn to confront your panic? Bear in mind that because you are human, previous learning will also be playing a large part in whether or not you flee the situation. Keep in mind also that avoidance in response to panic is only one way in which you avoid; you also avoid situations that you *anticipate* could lead to panic. Though flight is an automatic response to your first panic attack, especially if it is severe, it is not an automatic response to events for which you are prepared. The circumstances are analogous to your walking in a room, armed with a rifle, where you know a tiger lurks. Your anxiety is still there, but you are prepared to deal with it.

Early Learning

Early learning prepares the way for avoidance behavior. We learn by watching: children learn how to respond to stress by watching their parents respond to stress. If your parents react to stress by running away from it, you will learn to react to stress by running away from it. If your parents make excuses for not engaging in various activities, you, when confronted with the anxiety of engaging in such activities, will also find an arsenal of excuses at your disposal—learned from your parents. As an example, consider again the case of Ruth. Ruth remembers being very attached to her father, a binge drinker whose job history was a succession of crises, usually confrontations by his boss over some inadequacy in his performance. Ruth's father responded to such criticism by quitting his job, a decision that triggered another drinking bout. Even though Ruth hated her father's pattern of behavior, she inevitably learned that the way to deal with criticism was to run from it. And Ruth is not unusual; we frequently find in our repertoires the very traits of our parents that we admire the least.

The Impact of Language. The very language you have learned to use affects your perceptions and cognitions, in turn affecting your actions. Consider the use of expressions such as "going crazy," "losing control," and "falling apart" to describe the physical symptoms of a panic attack. These expressions represent not literal descriptions of the physical symptoms of a panic attack, but highly vivid and symbolic conclusions about what seems to be happening. I have asked a number of people what they meant in describing themselves as "falling apart" during a panic attack. Many have responded by describing images of their bodies disintegrating, or, in some cases, their brains decomposing. Their choice of the phrase "falling apart" seemed to prepare them to interpret their response to stress as their bodies falling apart. The same is true of the words used to describe avoidance behavior. "I've got to get out of here" and "I can't handle this" suggest an absolute necessity to avoid a situation. Such thoughts permit no choice and no examination of the consequences. Often, this use of language can be traced to your childhood. Repeatedly hearing your parents describe various behaviors as "crazy" or "out of control" teaches you to describe those or similar behaviors in the same way as an adult. This is true regardless of whether your parents are describing their own behavior, other people's behavior, or your behavior.

Reward and Punishment. Parental patterns of reward and punishment teach you to avoid or confront stress. The rewards and punishments you experience as a child also affect both your way of thinking and whether or not you will attempt to escape and avoid stressful situations. Being rewarded for escapist behavior and punished for assertive and problem-solving behavior lead to a general tendency to avoid stress: you have learned that things will be better if you avoid challenging situations. Further, if you are not encouraged to think through events that arouse anxiety, you develop no skills in finding better solutions. When faced with a stressful experience, you revert to the pattern of behavior you have learned best: escape.

Females are ten times more likely than males to adopt avoidance strategies in response to panic attacks. Why should this be so? The answer appears to lie in the way parents—because of social norms—respond to stress reactions in boys and girls. A boy who is upset over some event is typically told to go back and face the source of his distress. A girl in the same circumstances is typically comforted and not encouraged or instructed to return and face her distress. Repeated again and again, the message is clear: Boys, face your challenges or else. Girls, avoiding uncomfortable situations is OK. When panic strikes in adulthood, the ingrained message is the easiest to listen to.

Messages to a child, if repeated frequently enough, are likely to be assimilated. Messages like "When faced with a difficulty, give up or turn to others to solve your problem" are general enough to apply to a variety of situations. When the situation is a panic attack, the automatic response will inevitably be to give up. Further, a number of panic attack sufferers, especially those who have begun avoiding circumstances that they associate with previous attacks, have been shown to seek out and develop dependent relationships with others. They also have been shown to attribute events in their lives to circumstances outside of their control. This, however, seems to be true only of positive and problem-solving experiences; panic attack victims seem to have learned that negative events are inevitably their fault.

Again, this way of thinking often comes from a pattern of early learning that teaches you to look inside for reasons when you have failed and to give credit to others when you have succeeded. Taught, on the one hand, to be humble about your successes and not sing your own praises, you are taught, on the other, to admit your faults. Such contradictions pave the way for you to view your panic episodes as a failure of character while simultaneously denigrating your efforts to deal with these attacks.

What Are You Avoiding?

Identifying the degree to which you currently avoid situations will give you a standard against which to determine how your treatment program is progressing. To assess your current degree of avoidance, complete the Avoidance Questionnaire in Table 9.1. Simply rate each of the situations according to whether or not you avoided it in the last week, using the scale provided. Then total your points to get one overall score. As your treatment progresses, especially as you begin applying coping strategies in places you previously avoided or in

Table 9.1 Avoidance Questionnaire

Instructions: People with panic and anxiety often find it difficult to enter specific situations. Listed below are a number of commonly avoided situations. Please rate each situation as to how often in the last week you avoided it because of panic or anxiety. Use the following scale:

1 = did not avoid or escape
2 = occasionally avioded or escaped
3 = sometimes avoided; was able to enter alone
4 = usually avoided; rarely entered alone; had to be accompanied
5 = always avoided; did not enter even with a "safe person"

Drove	____
Rode in car	____
Went to grocery store	____
Went to mall	____
Was in crowds	____
Traveled by bus	____
Flew in airplane	____
Rode in taxicab	____
Waited in line	____
Walked outside your home	____
Rode in elevators	____
Was at home	____
Sat in movie theaters	____
Ate in restaurants	____
Went to theaters	____
Sat in auditoriums	____
Went to church	____
Drove through tunnels	____
Was in small rooms	____
Went to parks	____
Went to work	____
Was alone	____
Sat in dentist's chair	____
Went to strange cities	____
Went to barber shops	____
Went to beautician's shop	____
Went to social gatherings	____
Total	____

which you felt anxious, your avoidance score should drop. For this particular scale, how your score compares to that of others with panic disorder is not important. What is important is to determine whether or not your avoidance pattern is improving as a result of treatment.

Identifying what types of situations you most often avoid may provide clues about the fear underlying your avoidance. Once you understand your fear, you can examine it more clearly.

What, if anything, do the situations in Table 9.1 have in common? We can distinguish three themes. The first theme is common to public situations such as restaurants, auditoriums, and checkout lines. If you avoid such places, it is usually because you fear some form of social sanction, whether it be ridicule, disapproval, or rejection. One client I'll call Helen was explaining why her panic attacks were so paralyzing: she thought that she would choke to death during an attack. Thinking I had found the basis of her fear, I wondered aloud what about choking to death frightened her so much. Helen carefully explained that if she were to choke to death, people would wonder what on earth was wrong with her, and she would be terribly embarrassed.

Panic attacks produce a variety of symptoms that are associated with losing control in an ungraceful manner. Light-headedness, for example, is a prelude to fainting. If you experience light-headedness in a checkout line, you're likely to become concerned about fainting and about being laughed at or thought mentally deranged if you do. Expecting such a response, you naturally think to avoid the circumstances in which that response is most likely—the checkout line. The possibility that people would respond with concern and caring does not, of course, enter your mind.

The second theme is common to being in a dentist's chair, barber's chair, classroom, and so forth, where you feel trapped by the physical and social circumstances. In such circumstances, you fear that you will have a panic attack and be forced by circumstances not to take care of yourself but to respond in a socially conforming fashion. Take, for example, being in a dentist's chair. You begin to feel hot and faint and your heart is beating rapidly. Though going outside for some fresh air would relieve your symptoms, you feel trapped by the circumstances. How can you possibly get up to take care of yourself? You think of telling your dentist that you are mentally ill or suffer from a panic disorder as justification for going outside, but these thoughts only intensify your sense of being trapped. The possibility of simply saying, without explanation, that you need to go outside for some fresh air does not occur to you. Better to start filling your own cavities. This fear differs from the first because your trapped feeling is less related to embarrassment than to feeling unable to get out to deal with your anxiety.

The third theme, typical of avoiding driving and being alone, is fearing that you will be unable to get help during a panic attack because your panic will incapacitate you. This theme is likely operating in those who avoid strange cities, where not knowing how to get help, the victim could be stranded during a panic attack. It is also the rationale for not driving on interstate highways or roads where the distance between safe refuges, such as homes or service stations, is perceived to be great. In such situations, catastrophic thoughts of being trapped in your car with a never-ending panic attack and of the impossibility of medical intervention in the event of a heart attack or stroke are likely to surface. Again, the fact that thousands of motorists as well as police in cruisers travel these roads does not occur to you. Better to drive the back roads and enjoy the scenery.

The fear of being trapped, embarrassed, or helpless can be symbolic of what is going on in your life; that is, if you find yourself trying to avoid situations in which you feel trapped, examine broader areas of your life in which you feel trapped. Men and women who feel trapped in marriages, other relationships, or jobs and who experience panic attacks will go to great lengths to avoid physical circumstances that increase their feeling trapped. Likewise, avoiding embarrassment is often an expression of a life in which avoiding disapproval is a prevailing theme.

Take Tom, for example, a man who was intent on climbing to the top of the corporate ladder. The means he had unconsciously chosen to get to the top was to ingratiate himself with all who were influential. Without knowing it, he had made a bargain with himself to be the perfect employee, one for whom no breach of character or the work ethic was permissible. So that Tom would know when he was behaving imperfectly, he constantly scanned his environment for signs of disapproval by his colleagues and superiors. Seeking this information so ardently, he inevitably found it. Motivated by his own drive to succeed, he pushed himself to the point where he began experiencing panic attacks. His avoidance of every situation in which he had an attack was fueled by his obsession to be perfect, at least in the eyes of everyone else. Not surprisingly, he eventually began—subtly and secretly, of course—avoiding a variety of social situations in which he was afraid people would look down on him should he develop a panic attack in their presence.

It is not unusual for people using avoidance behavior to deal with their avoidance secretly. Why should this occur? Because you're embarrassed and ashamed of the lengths to which you'll go to avoid anxiety-provoking situations. In addition, if you tell someone, such as your partner, you run the risk of being told to confront the situation you fear. Here again, you are in a quandary. You've given yourself that same instruction, but you haven't been able to follow it. Being told by someone else to confront the situation only reminds you that you've already failed. Hence, you feel safer keeping your avoidance a secret, a decision that in itself is an act of avoidance.

It's easy to see how one set of avoidance behaviors begets another. Only when you realize both that you're enacting this pattern and the power of this pattern of behavior do you become equipped to deal with it. In the next chapter, we will look at the specifics of dealing with—that is, eliminating—this disruptive pattern of behavior.

Summary

Let's summarize how and why escape and avoidance behavior develops:

1. Panic is unpleasant, and you will automatically seek ways of reducing it. Over the short run, escape and avoidance reduce it. They work!
2. Deciding that you will not enter certain situations also reduces anticipatory anxiety.
3. Panic is a survival mechanism that signals the presence of danger. Fleeing, in turn, is an adaptive response to feelings of panic.
4. Having fled, you thereafter associate fleeing with both your feelings of panic and the situation itself. Repeating the experience several times fixes the learning in your memory and increases the chances that you will continue your avoidance.
5. Your chances of trying to avoid stressful situations when experiencing panic symptoms are higher if, in early learning, you (a) saw others avoid stressful situations, (b) were encouraged to avoid and rewarded for avoiding stressful situations, and (c) were discouraged from and punished for confronting them.
6. Perceiving the panic as caused by unknown forces and dealing with it as something outside of your control ensures that you will make no active attempt to cope with the problem.

Let's see how these factors can be neutralized by an active coping program.

10

Eliminating Avoidance Strategies

We have just examined what avoidance strategies are and how they develop. Avoidance behavior can be relatively mild, confined to such activities as avoiding driving long distances alone, or extreme, as when you avoid leaving the house or leave only when accompanied by another person. Such avoidance obviously restricts your life, sometimes severely. We will now examine how to begin to eliminate your use of avoidance strategies so that you can lead a more complete, fulfilling life.

The first step in eliminating your avoidance behavior is to recognize it for what it is: an impediment to recovery. That's a strong statement, but one that is absolutely true.

You already know that avoidance is a part of the problem of your panic attacks. What you didn't know is that avoidance is keeping you from learning to deal with the panic attacks themselves. How does that happen? We have seen that avoidance is powerfully rewarding because it reduces both the anxiety of the panic attack itself and the anxiety of anticipating a panic attack. Anxiety is a motivator. As long as you are experiencing it, you are searching for a way to reduce it. If you avoid the source of your anxiety, however, your anxiety will subside, and your search for other coping strategies can cease.

If your panic attacks continue even after you have begun avoiding situations that resemble the one in which your first attack occurred, you most likely will begin to search for other situations to avoid in hopes of reducing your chances of having further panic attacks. Unfortunately, your leaving such situations eliminates even the possibility of your learning other skills with which to cope with your attacks.

What else happens when you leave the place in which you're having a panic attack or refuse to go to such a place at all? You prove to yourself that you can't handle it. I've asked a number of avoiders how they know they're unable to handle a panic attack. Their most frequent response? They know because they have to leave or something

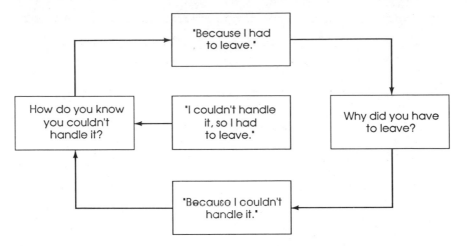

Figure 10.1 The circular thinking underlying avoidance strategies

terrible might happen. This is a perfect example of the circular think-ing characteristic of the avoidance response. There is no way out of this circle other than to stop leaving, which then proves that you didn't have to leave! Examine the reasoning illustrated in Figure 10.1. How often do you offer similar explanations for your behavior?

Short- and Long-Term Payoffs

There is an important distinction to be made between short-term and long-term payoffs in regard to avoidance: avoidance works over the short term; it is devastating over the long term. Confrontation is pain-ful over the short term; it pays off over the long term. Anxiety, espe-cially panic, can drive you to short-term solutions, but anxiety and panic are problems for which you need long-term strategies.

How is avoidance a good short-term strategy but bad in the long term? Research has shown that panic attack sufferers who use avoid-ance strategies are even more anxious than panic attack sufferers who do not use them. Other research has shown that as panic attack sufferers who avoid situations they fear begin to confront those situa-tions, their overall level of anxiety, as well as their anxiety in the situa-tions they previously avoided, begins to decrease. Such findings indicate quite clearly that avoidance does not work in the long term and that confrontation of one's fears does.

In one sense, avoidance strategies fail over the short term as well as the long term. Because avoidance represents a failure to confront a fear, both your self-esteem and self-efficacy suffer; you become immediately convinced of your inability to deal with fearful situations. So, avoidance as a short-term strategy really has only one payoff: it reduces your immediate sense of panic. In every other way, it is injurious to your mental health.

These arguments are aimed at starting a process that you must complete: assessing the role avoidance plays in your life, deciding to stop avoiding, and instituting the counterstrategies that will enable you to stop. Give careful thought to these arguments, because you must be convinced of their validity before you will be ready to decide to give up avoiding.

Deciding to Stop Avoiding

Deciding something once and for all is impossible. Often, the decision to do something must be made anew daily—at times, hourly. Consider the motto of Alcoholics Anonymous: "One day at a time." That motto reflects the recognition that one must decide to stop drinking repeatedly, in fact, daily. Deciding to confront situations you have been avoiding is the same way; do not be fooled into believing that such a decision need be made only once. I call one-shot decisions "New Year's resolutions," after those promises you make once a year and break the next day—or certainly no later than January 3. One reason such promises fail is that those making them do not recognize the difficulty of their undertaking and the need to make the same decision repeatedly.

Decisions to stop avoiding resemble New Year's resolutions in another way—namely, in their makers' belief that such decisions must be final, irreversible, and successful. The emphasis here is on success. This attitude is reflected in the expression "breaking" a New Year's resolution. The implication of saying that you've broken a resolution is that it is beyond repair—break a resolution once and you might just as well break it again. Once broken, a promise to yourself is no longer a promise. The only thing to do is wait until the next year to make a new resolution.

The New Year's resolution approach is completely counterproductive. It is also naive. Any habit is hard to change, and avoidance is one of the hardest. The only way to approach changing such a habit is to take it one day at a time.

We must distinguish here between agreeing to put yourself in a situation regardless of whether or not you experience panic and feeling no fear once you are in the situation. Success is not the absence of fear when you put yourself in a situation you have previously avoided. Success is simply being there! I therefore ask only that you agree to put yourself in the situation and that you ask of yourself nothing more than that. To ask yourself to feel no panic is unreason-able; ask only that you confront the situation you fear. Again, once you have decided to confront the situation, recognize that you may make that same decision 100 more times before you actually do it. You are going through an honest struggle, a struggle that helps you rehearse your confrontation. You can prepare extensively before ac-tually confronting a situation you have been avoiding.

Discovering Your "What Ifs"

When you decide to confront a situation you have been avoiding, you will discover a number of frightening questions. These are the "what ifs," and they represent what you most fear about your panic attacks. You already know some of your what ifs, but there are many others you need to discover so that you can begin to deal with them. This is best done by going on a fantasy trip, armed with a pad and pen, to the situation you have been avoiding.

Let's say that you've been avoiding restaurants, for instance. Imagine that you go to one. What thoughts do you have about what might hap-pen to you? *Without avoiding*, stay with the scene to find out other thoughts you might have about what could happen to you—what if questions. Write these questions down as they occur to you, and then return to your fantasy.

I used the following process to elicit questions from Mary, who was afraid of going into restaurants.

Me: Okay, Mary, imagine that you're contemplating whether or not to go for lunch at a restaurant. What do you think of?
Mary: I think, what if I have a panic attack?
Me: What would you do if you did?
Mary: I'd leave the restaurant.
Me: Imagine that you don't leave. What happens next?
Mary: I take a seat at a table, but I'm already beginning to feel strange.
Me: Pay attention to what's happening to you.
Mary: But what if thinking about it brings on a panic attack?
Me: Let yourself think about it and find out what happens.
Mary: OK, my heart is beating faster, and I'm having trouble breathing. So I think, what if I can't breathe?
Me: Then what happens?
Mary: I'm having trouble breathing.
Me: Then what do you think?
Mary: What if I have a panic attack and faint?
Me: Imagine you do; what would happen then?
Mary: People would be standing around looking at me and laughing.

Notice that the first what if Mary thought of was having a panic attack. She left out many of the symptoms and thoughts that would occur before she actually would have an attack. She did not consider the process of getting to and entering the restaurant or her thoughts during this period of time. Without knowing these events, she would be ill-equipped to deal with them if she tried to return to the restaurant without first going on a fantasy trip. Mary also learned in this process that she was afraid of fainting and then being ridiculed, two fears she had not previously connected with her fear of having a panic attack. Once she learned what some of her specific what ifs questions were, she was able to answer them.

Answering Your "What Ifs"

Mary's what ifs are among those most typically expressed by panic attack sufferers:

- What if I chicken out?
- What if I have a panic attack?
- What if I really do have a heart attack or a cerebral embolism and so on?
- What if I pass out?
- What if it doesn't stop?
- What if somebody, everybody, sees me?
- What if I really do go crazy?
- What if they call an ambulance (doctor, coroner)?
- What if I lose control and hit someone (hurt someone, kill someone)?
- What if I die?

Interestingly, what ifs never get answered, and so they loom as possibilities and remain persuasive reasons for avoiding the feared situation. The best strategy for dealing with what if questions is to answer them rationally.

- If I chicken out, I can try again. After all, I've already recognized that I'll have setbacks.
- If I have a panic attack, I won't be surprised. Moreover, I have a number of strategies for dealing with a panic attack.
- If I really do have a heart attack, I or someone else will call a doctor. If I'm wrong and it's not really a heart attack, I'll have made an honest mistake.
- If I pass out, I'll probably feel it coming and can position myself so I don't get hurt when I fall. If people are standing around watching me when I come to, I'll ask them to move so I can get some air.

- If it doesn't stop, I guess I'll eventually have to be taken to a hospital, but I have a lot of strategies to try before that happens. I have no experience that says it will never stop, and I'll have to trust my experience.
- If everybody sees me, I'll have to remind myself that I really don't know what they're thinking about me and it's irrational to think that I do.

It is naive, of course, to think that what ifs can be answered with a single response. Any one what if really represents a series of what ifs connected to it. The entire series must be answered before you will feel that solutions really exist to the scenarios that fuel your terror.

Another thing to remember is that what ifs cause a great deal of anxiety, thus increasing the chance that you will think illogically. Writing down your answers to your what ifs is therefore essential, so that you can remember that you do have logical and realistic answers. Having these answers with you in a fearful situation so that you can read them when you start asking your what if questions can be useful.

You will inevitably discover when you confront the actual situation you fear that you have not anticipated all of the possible questions you can scare yourself by asking. Like any proving ground, the actual situation will demonstrate the flaws in your preparation. You have to use that proving ground to discover the hidden what ifs in your scenario and then answer whatever additional ones you find. Don't patronize yourself by giving answers that you recognize as nonsense. Give yourself logical, realistic answers that you can believe in.

Let's follow an internal what if conversation of Judy, who feared having a panic attack while driving.

Judy had not driven a car on a highway for seven years. She had only recently allowed herself to try driving on city streets and had managed to drive 17 miles on back roads to seek psychotherapy for her anxiety attacks. She had been hospitalized for depression ten years before and was terrified that she might have to be hospitalized again. Hence, she feared that driving would bring on a panic attack that would culminate in her being hospitalized. Being hospitalized, in turn, represented being helpless and out of control. She had the following conversation with herself:

Judy's fear: I can't drive on highways.
Judy: Why not?
Her fear: I might lose control and crash.
Judy: What do you mean by "lose control"?
Her fear: Well, what if I had a panic attack, couldn't control myself, and lost control of the car?
Judy: Let me ask you a question. What makes you think that these symptoms would make you lose control of the car? They never have, have they?

Her fear: No. But what if they do?

Judy: What symptoms make you think you're going to lose control?

Her fear: Well, first, my heart starts pounding really fast. Then I feel light-headed and have a hard time breathing, and I think I'm going to pass out. I feel really weird and not in control of the car.

Judy: So the light-headed feeling is preceded by your heart pounding. You have strategies for dealing with that. And if you were to become light-headed, what would you do?

Her fear: Well, I could roll down the windows or sing loudly.

Judy: Yes, these are things that you can do. Have you tried them in the past and have they worked?

Her fear: I've used them before. Sometimes they work and sometimes they don't. But what if it got worse?

Judy: What would you do if it got worse?

Her fear: I could pull over to the side of the road.

Judy: That's right.

Her fear: But what if it didn't get better?

Judy: What could you do if it didn't get better?

Her fear: I could wave down another motorist or walk to the nearest house. But what if the nearest house were miles away?

Judy: You'd have a long walk ahead of you!

The foregoing internal conversation is typical of the kind I encourage if you are avoiding some situation because you fear that you will have a panic attack in it. The what ifs yield to a straightforward confrontation about what you can do in a variety of scenarios.

Responding to Ultimate "What Ifs"

Sometimes a what if scenario leads to an ultimate event such as death or permanent confinement in a mental hospital. Several responses to these what ifs are possible. One possible response is to examine the likelihood of such an event; after doing so, most people agree that such an event is highly unlikely. Take, for example, the fear that a panic attack can kill you. Some possible responses include:

- I know that no one ever died from a panic attack.
- I need to examine how I think a panic attack will kill me and see whether that is likely or not. If I think I'll stop breathing, for example, I need to remind myself that I have voluntary control over my breathing. If I pass out, my automatic response will be to continue to breathe. If I think my heart will stop, I need to remind myself that my pulse getting slow or faint does not mean my heart will stop. It is my body's way of regulating itself. If I think my heart will explode, I need to remind myself that hearts don't explode. Heart attacks occur when the arteries that supply oxygen to the heart close.

This closing is something that occurs over a long period of time. A second possible response you can make addresses the irrational fear that you really may die or really may go insane forever. Even when you know that such outcomes are unlikely, and even when you know that such fears are the products of panic, remnants of these fears may persist. They then require more careful examination, as follows:

1. Discover the fear behind the fear. People who fear death or insanity have a mental image of these states. Behind the fear of death may be the fear of the pain of dying or of being separated from people you love. Behind the fear of mental illness may be the fear of being out of touch with reality or locked in the back wards of a mental institution.

2. Once you know the precise basis for your fear, examine the connection between your symptoms and the outcome you fear. Does thinking that your panic attack symptoms, whether they be rapid heart rate, difficulty breathing, or the like, will lead to pain beyond all your experience or to being out of touch with reality make sense?

3. Ultimately, of course, you will have to deal with the reality of death. You may also have to deal with senility. These are natural concerns for which people prepare throughout their lives. Remind yourself of whatever preparations you have made and of how you will actually cope with these situations. Ask yourself if you cannot face up to these situations and identify ways of doing so. Once you adopt this point of view, the calamity you fear will prove less of a calamity precisely because you fear it less.

Rehearsing Your Confrontation

Once you have decided to confront a situation you have been avoiding and have composed responses to your what if questions, you are ready to begin rehearsing your confrontation. Rehearsing involves fantasizing, step-by-step, how you will accomplish confronting your fear.

To do this, you need to find a quiet, comfortable place where you can be alone. Sit in a comfortable chair, and relax using one of the strategies described in Chapter 5. You are the expert; use whichever technique works best for you. All of this preparation is necessary to induce a state in which your images will be crystal clear.

When you are relaxed and ready, mentally rehearse your confrontation according to the following steps:

1. Imagine the situation you fear.
2. Confront it in your imagination; that is, imagine yourself in that situation.

3. Examine the thoughts and feelings you experience in response to being there, being sure to separate the two.
4. Cope with both your thoughts and your feelings by answering any what ifs that come up.
5. Proceed to the next group of symptoms and thoughts you would likely experience in that situation.
6. Repeat the process described in steps 3 through 5 of examining and coping with your symptoms and thoughts.

To assist you in your mental rehearsal, I recommend that you tape-record your imagined confrontation; you can then play it back to yourself repeatedly. Record the following four things:

1. a description of the physical circumstances you will be confronting;
2. a description of your thoughts in that situation and your thoughts in response to your general physiological changes;
3. a description of the physiological changes themselves (changes in your heart rate, breathing rate or difficulty, temperature, and so forth); and
4. your answers to the what if questions at each point at which they arise.

Using fantasy is valuable because your problem basically stems from your fantasy or perception of what will happen. You can control fantasy in that you decide what will happen in the fantasy and how you will deal with what happens. If you can deal with the problem in fantasy, you can deal with it in reality. Bill Fosbury, inventor of the Fosbury Flop, a method of high jumping in which one goes over the bar backward, used to fantasize for up to a half hour before he attempted a jump. He would imagine himself going over the bar successfully and would think through each of his body's responses at each point in the jump. He was then ready to approach the high jump. The fantasy process outlined here allows you to similarly rehearse both your physical and cognitive responses to the situation before actually putting yourself in it.

Your first fantasy confrontation will be the most difficult, because the process generates considerable anxiety, exactly what you have been trying to prevent. Furthermore, since avoidance is familiar and confrontation is not, you may find imagining yourself successfully confronting your fear quite difficult. You may also find coping with your responses difficult, simply because solving problems is difficult when you're feeling anxious. Accordingly, I recommend that you first practice some of the coping strategies outlined in Chapters 5 and 7 and have some experience with them before you embark on confronting your avoidance, even in imagination.

Two final steps remain for you in learning to confront your avoidance. The first is to repeat the fantasy over and over until you can get through the fantasy without a great deal of anxiety. You should feel confident that you can handle, in fantasy, the situation you fear, your thoughts, and your feelings.

You are then ready for the second stage—actually confronting the situation. But keep this in mind: though ready for the actual confrontation, you will inevitably doubt yourself, wondering if the reality won't be totally different from your fantasy and if you will fall on your face when in the situation itself. That's an understandable fear, one that everyone shares. Don't expect that you will experience no anxiety. You will! Don't expect that you won't have a panic attack. You might! The difference will be that this time you will not run but rather will use it as an opportunity to find out more about your attacks and how you deal with them. Think of your first return to the situation you fear as a trial run after your initial training. You have not yet been field-tested. The field tests will point out additional problems. With each confrontation in the field, however, as with each fantasized confrontation, you will gain confidence in your ability to deal with the situation. You are on your way to recovery.

Confronting the Situations You Avoid

Once you feel comfortable confronting in fantasy the situations you have been avoiding, you are ready to take on the real thing. Here is a prescription for a successful confrontation:

1. Make a detailed list of situations you avoid. This list should specify the circumstances of the situations you avoid. For example, suppose you avoid driving but not under all circumstances. You specifically avoid driving (a) by yourself, (b) on interstate highways, (c) at night, (d) when it is raining, and (e) in places which are unfamiliar to you. The worst possible scenario would be driving under all of the above circumstances. Further, some combinations would be more frightening than others, and some might feel relatively safe—driving around the block by yourself at night, for instance.

2. Rank these situations according to how much they frighten you. Use a scale of 1 to 10 to indicate how much anxiety each situation arouses, with 1 representing no anxiety and 10 the most anxiety you've ever felt. Be sure that you have included on your list situations of all degrees of fearfulness—those that, though you occasionally avoid them, feel relatively safe; those that you find more frightening and avoid more frequently; those that you usually avoid; and those that you always avoid.

3. Referring to your ranking, and starting with the situation with which you feel most confident in dealing (most likely the situation you have ranked number 1), place yourself in that actual situation.

4. While in this situation, let yourself imagine the symptoms and thoughts that have scared you before. Practice coping with your symptoms and your thoughts as they occur. Though these symptoms and thoughts should be pretty similar to those you rehearsed in your imagination, you may experience additional symptoms and thoughts once you are in the actual situation.

5. Do not criticize yourself for any imagined failure in this process. Do reward yourself by acknowledging and congratulating yourself for your efforts.

6. Proceed to the next situation on your list and repeat the process.

You will find that the going is slow at first. You may feel that you are not succeeding as much as you wished to. This is to be expected. As you learn to cope with the first few situations, your confidence will grow with increasing speed. You may even want to skip some of the situations in your hierarchy, confident in your ability to deal with them. That is perfectly reasonable and does not constitute a risk to the program. Further, some situations may be relatively rare and therefore difficult to reproduce. You should recognize this at the outset as a limitation in your retraining program.

As with imaginal practice, you will benefit the most from confronting the situations you avoid if you do it on a daily basis. If circumstances other than your own make confronting those situations daily impossible, strive to practice as close to daily as possible. The more often you confront the situations you fear, the stronger the message that you can confront them will be.

What if the nature of the situations you avoid makes confronting them daily or even weekly impossible? Airplane flights are one such example. Can you still overcome your avoidance? The answer is still "Yes, you can!" What is important is that you confront what you normally avoid *when the opportunity presents itself.* If you fear and avoid driving alone and you confront that fear and avoidance on weekends only, while avoiding driving during the rest of the week, your progress will be slow at best. To succeed in your program of confrontation, you must actively engage your fears at every opportunity.

Determining how long to stay in a situation you have previously avoided is also important. There is no easy answer to this, since circumstances determine how long you stay in many situations. Your guiding principle should be to experience success: you should remain in each situation long enough for you to experience a reduction—not necessarily an elimination—in your anxiety while in the situation. This will help you come to connect your efforts and the satisfaction success brings.

Once you begin experiencing success in confronting your fears, hammer the lesson home. By this I mean seize every opportunity to confront the situation—invent excuses, if necessary. One of my clients who had panic attacks in public situations in which he felt he was the center of attention became a weekly reader at his place of worship and joined Toastmasters, an organization for developing public speaking skills. In another case, a student afraid of panicking in elevators took to riding the elevator at every opportunity; when he could choose between walking down a flight of stairs or taking the elevator, he chose the elevator. Using this approach maximizes your likelihood of overcoming your avoidance, not just to the point of being able to tolerate those situations but to the point of feeling comfortable in them.

Distinguishing Coping from Avoiding

How can you distinguish between subtle, self-defeating avoidance behaviors and coping strategies such as distraction or gradual exposure to the situation you fear? You will know when you are conning yourself. If you are conning yourself, you will come out of your confrontation with a diminished feeling of success, knowing that you avoided your fear and that you are not coping in a way that leads to long-term gains. Some examples of positive coping strategies will help clarify the distinction between subtle avoidance and some common-sense coping strategies.

- You go to a smoke-filled restaurant. You know you have difficulty breathing in such an environment, so you select a part of the room with the least smoke. It happens to be the table nearest the door.
- You are in a checkout line when you feel faint. You tell the salesclerk that you're feeling faint but to check you out while you go outside to get some air. You get some air and return for your groceries.
- You decide to go to a shopping mall at the least busy time of day, not because you fear your response to a crowd, but because you'll get your shopping done faster.

As the second example shows, coping with anxiety sometimes means leaving a situation temporarily. That your actions weren't avoidance in this example is evident in the fact that you returned to the store for your groceries. In the first and third examples, the motives and the self-examination involved make these choices reasonable coping devices rather than avoidance.

Taking care of yourself is certainly sensible. The ability to acknowledge that you have legitimate preferences is part of the process of learning to cope effectively with stress. Though avoidance has as a motive the reduction of anxiety, it also leaves you feeling as though you are not dealing effectively with the situation. In fact, you arc not: you can't learn new coping skills if you never enter the situation with which you need to learn to cope.

There is another way of knowing whether or not your coping response is really avoidance. Take the example of shopping when few people are in the store. How do you know if you are exercising a simple preference instead of avoiding crowds? The answer is simple: if you can, at times, shop comfortably when stores are crowded but choose to shop on some occasions when they aren't, you are exercising a simple preference; if you cannot, you are avoiding.

Cognitive Avoidance

In addition to behavioral avoidance is the phenomenon of cognitive avoidance. Cognitive avoidance is especially problematic, because of its subtlety and its tendency to undermine success. To the person beginning to confront situations he or she has previously avoided, it can serve as a last-ditch attempt to preserve the avoidance strategy.

How does cognitive avoidance work? Having put yourself in the situation you fear, you reduce your anxiety by avoiding examining your environment, your thoughts, or your feelings. Some examples:

- In a checkout line you have previously avoided, fearing that the salesclerk is watching you, you avert your eyes so that you don't meet his or hers.
- When the thought that you are going crazy intrudes, you refuse to examine it lest you begin to believe you are going crazy.
- When confronting a difficult situation, you tell yourself before, during, and afterward that you only did it because you were told to.

I could cite many more examples. They all involve playing a mind game with yourself in which you always lose. "True," you say to yourself, "I am confronting my fear. But I am confronting it in a way that is really cheating."

How can you counter cognitive avoidance? The first thing to do is to recognize what you are doing and how you are undermining your own treatment program. Cognitive avoidance is just another form of avoidance, after all. The second thing to do is to take responsibility for your improvement. This means deciding to fully confront the situations you avoid, any symptoms that occur, and your cata-strophic thoughts. Having decided to confront those situations fully, you can then mentally rehearse your confrontation and put it into practice.

Dealing with Setbacks

The first tactic to use in dealing with setbacks is to realize what a setback is *not*. Having a panic attack when you confront a situation you have been avoiding is not a setback. Doubting your ability to deal with the situation is not a setback. Using a coping strategy that may be mistaken for avoidance is not a setback.

A setback *is* leaving the situation you are in while you are in the midst of a panic attack and not returning to deal with the situation. We saw that you can take care of yourself by temporarily leaving a situation to deal with your panic symptoms. It makes sense, as we have seen, to leave a checkout line, get some fresh air, and then return to retrieve your groceries. It makes sense to pull off the road if you're feeling dizzy and your vision has blurred, to relax and regain your composure before resuming driving. Only when you leave your gro-ceries and go home, or call someone to pick you up should you con-sider that you have had a setback.

Having a setback should tell you something: you are trying to run before you can walk. You have pushed your training program beyond your ability to cope. The solution is to retrace your steps. Perhaps all you need do is return to imagining yourself confronting the situation in which your setback has occurred, rebuild your sense of confidence in your strategies, and confront the situation again. If you follow this course, you must retrace in imagination the events that occurred when you confronted the actual situation and experienced the setback. Iden-tify the point at which you decided to escape and figure out a way to cope with the situation without avoiding. In this way, you use your setback to gain the additional information you need to ultimately succeed.

A second approach to a setback is to return to a less fearful situa-tion on your avoidance list, one that you have confronted successfully and that you are confident of confronting successfully again. Remem-ber that a setback is likely to produce a crisis in confidence, and that you may have a tendency to denigrate your previous accomplishments. If you need to return to a situation earlier in the hierarchy, be sure to use your imagination again to prepare yourself for the encounter.

Let's now look in some detail at a client who had a history—before coming to our clinic—of seeking out treatment with varying levels of success. After some improvement, but not complete success, she would end treatment. After a while, she would experience a return of her attacks and return to treatment. Her case affords us an opportunity to examine some causes of attacks and how to deal with them.

A Case History

Setbacks come in many shapes and sizes. Sometimes they come when you shift from one stage of treatment to another, such as when you progress from confronting situations in your imagination to confronting them in reality. Sometimes setbacks come for no identifiable reason. You seem to be doing fine, and—WHAM—all of a sudden you're doing lousy. Such setbacks can be the hardest to deal with, since you cannot explain them. At other times, setbacks come after you've successfully completed your treatment program. Usually, in such cases, some event has occurred to stress you. It is best to be prepared for such events, for it is then that you can suffer a setback. What can you do to prepare for a setback? Let's look at the case of Frances.

Frances had been in therapy before for her panic disorder. In fact, she had seen several physicians, who had treated her with medication, and a couple of psychologists, who had treated her with psychotherapy. Frances had also developed a moderately severe pattern of avoidance—she avoided restaurants, shopping malls, and other places that she could expect to be crowded—and since none of her previous treatments targeted this problem, she continued to avoid. Each of the medication and psychotherapy regimens had helped, in that her panic attacks were greatly reduced, though never eliminated. After each of the treatments ended, Frances would experience a period of relative calm, lasting from a couple of months to a year. With each new flare-up, however, Frances became increasingly disenchanted and discouraged. She began to believe that she had no hope of eliminating her attacks.

When Frances came to our clinic with her sixth "relapse," my colleagues and I, in conjunction with Frances, outlined the following goals and strategies:

Goals

1. Reduce the frequency of the panic attacks and the severity of the symptoms.
2. Eliminate the catastrophic cognitions associated with the panic attacks.

Strategies

1. Diaphragmatic breathing, relaxation exercises, and cognitive restructuring.
2. Reviewing information about the attacks, cognitive restructuring both while relaxed and while having panic symptoms.

3. Eliminate the avoidance behavior.

3. Imaginal and actual confrontation of the avoided situations,
   implementation of strategies
   for coping with symptoms and
   thoughts while in avoided situations.

4. Develop the belief that panic
   attacks are not catastrophic
   and that many things can be
   done to control them.

4. Practicing having panic attacks by bringing on symptoms through hyperventilation
   in previously avoided situations.

Because Frances came to us believing that her previous therapies
had failed, we were careful to show her that she had, in fact, been
helped each time. The problems with her previous therapies were that
(1) she had not dealt successfully with all her problems, especially
her avoidance; (2) she had believed a cure to be in the hands of the
professionals treating her, not her own; and (3) she had defined a cure
as having "no further problems." In helping her to understand and
appreciate the extent to which she had succeeded previously, we were
able to raise her expectations for additional improvement as well as
help her anticipate that setbacks and recurrences were part and parcel
of the problem.

Treatment did not go smoothly. Each time she was to confront a
situation she avoided, Frances would begin rationalizing that she
really did not need to learn to confront it, that, after all, she had survived this long without constant confrontation. In addition, she would
begin to claim that avoiding this situation wasn't the problem after
all. In essence, she didn't have to overcome the problem, since there
was no problem. Her panic attacks invariably increased before she
was to confront a new situation, and she would plead to take time
to reduce the attacks before having to confront it. We dealt with this
simply: "It's your choice," we said, "but if you want to get better, you
must decide to confront the situation." Frances consistently chose to
continue treatment and go ahead with her confrontation. We also explained that her increased panic attacks provided her an excellent
opportunity to learn to deal with flare-ups and setbacks. We urged
her to turn apparent defeat into certain victory just by thinking about
it differently. Reluctantly, it seemed, Frances complied, but always
with a hint that she wasn't totally buying our definition of her problem and its solution.

We terminated treatment when Frances seemed to have improved
as much as she was going to. She still avoided certain situations, and
she still believed that proper treatment would eliminate her attacks
once and forever. Prior to entering treatment, she had left a job she

considered too stressful, and at the end of treatment, she still believed she was mentally unready to return to full-time employment.

During the following year, Frances had infrequent attacks about once every two months but felt able to control them. In fact, she felt increasingly confident in her ability to control her attacks—so much so that she decided to return to full-time work. About a week before returning to work, Frances experienced a significant increase in the frequency of her attacks, though she noted that they were less severe than before. She reentered treatment at our clinic.

Though Frances was slightly discouraged, we were not. We asked her the following questions:

Therapist: Why do you think the attacks returned?

Frances: Because I had decided to return to work, and I was worried that I couldn't handle it.

Therapist: Do you think your decision to return to work represented weakness or strength?

Frances: Strength. I thought I could handle it.

Therapist: Are you handling it?

Frances: To some extent, but the attacks have returned.

Therapist: Did you anticipate that your attacks might return if you went back to work?

Frances: I thought it was a possibility. But I didn't want to stay home forever.

Therapist: So, knowing you were risking the return of your attacks, you went back to work regardless!

Frances: Yes!

Therapist: What do you think that means in terms of your being afraid of your attacks?

Frances: I guess I'm less afraid of my attacks than I am of not working for the rest of my life.

Therapist: Good!

For someone like Frances, discouraged over what are perceived as therapeutic failures, to doubt that any treatment can really help is not unusual. Once she redefined for herself what was meant by help and accepted that panic attacks can return, Frances was able to deal with her setbacks in an increasingly realistic fashion. Her return to work represented a dramatic new belief that she could handle both a situation she had previously avoided and the return of her panic attacks. Her return to treatment represented not another failure but a realistic appraisal that she needed help to deal with her difficult situation.

This case demonstrates three important steps in dealing with setbacks:

1. Understand and anticipate the type of situations likely to increase your panic.

2. Expect that panic attacks will return and that they may return when you least expect them. Recognize that occasional panic attacks are not cause for alarm but are reason to reinstitute your coping strategies.

3. If the return of panic attacks takes you by surprise, review the circumstances leading up to it. You are likely to find that their return was understandable.

Resistance to Change

People give a number of seemingly plausible reasons for not acting to change their panic disorder. Let's look at some of these reasons and ways in which you can think about and deal with them.

1. *Imagining something isn't the same as the real thing!* Of course not—but it's pretty close! First of all, as you already recognize, what you fear is really in you. All you have to do to feel anxious is think about having an attack or being in a situation you fear. You don't have to actually be in the situation; your memory of it will suffice to make you anxious. Your anxiety attacks are, in fact, portable: you carry them around with you. They come not from the situation, but from you. If you can learn to imagine all of the things that frighten you without becoming frightened, two things will have happened. You won't become scared while thinking about them, and you'll reduce your chances of being scared when you actually encounter them. Furthermore, you're not simply relying on imagining the situations that scare you to reduce your panic; you're using these sessions to prepare yourself to confront the real thing.

2. *But when I imagine it, I don't even feel anxious!* A couple of mechanisms may be operating here, but you're right in assuming that if you're not experiencing any anxiety when imagining situations that normally scare you, imagination is not likely to help. One possibility is that your mental images are not clear. Just as you can learn to drive, you can learn to imagine clearly, but it takes practice. You must remember also to imagine not only the situations in which you experience anxiety but also your actual anxious response. You have to let yourself feel it. If that's too frightening for you, have someone available to support you when you're practicing your imagery. Remember that even though most people who have panic attacks are typically good imagers, for some, becoming a good imager takes practice.

3. *My problems are more complex than just avoiding things.* Of course they're more complex than that. But you have to start with one problem at a time, and since the problem interfering most with your life is your avoidance of activities necessary to live a full life, it makes

sense to start by learning to cope with the situations you fear and avoid. Your avoidance gets you in trouble, not only with yourself but also with important people in your life. You need to deal with your avoidance first, so you can see how much of your trouble comes from avoidance and how much comes from other things.

4. *If I could just understand why I'm this way, maybe it would go away.* It is important for you to understand what factors may have led you to develop panic attacks, but that understanding will not make them go away. No matter how well you understand your panic, you still have to face it and the situations that cause it, and doing that is tough. Furthermore, simply understanding why something has happened can serve as an excuse for not changing it. This is the "poor me" syndrome. There's only one way to feel that you can do something: do it!

5. *I can't do it alone.* For some people, doing it alone is too difficult at first. You may need to obtain the assistance of a spouse or trusted friend. You may also need to find a trained professional to help you overcome your problem. In any case, help is temporary. Ultimately, it is you who must face the situation you fear, and you must face it alone.

Summary

Let's summarize what you need to do to eliminate your pattern of avoidance:

1. You must first acknowledge that if you continue to avoid situations you fear, your panic disorder will also continue. Further, since avoidance successfully reduces anxiety, you run the risk of avoiding more and more situations and having your world shrink tighter and tighter.
2. Think of avoidance as a short-term coping strategy. Let yourself realize that you need a long-term approach to your problem.
3. Arm yourself with information on panic attacks and ways of coping with both the symptoms and the thoughts that accompany them.
4. Use fantasy to discover your what if questions. Make a written list of these questions.
5. Answer your what if questions.
6. Practice some of the various coping strategies and gain some experience with them.
7. Use your panic attack fantasy to develop a full scenario of the various things you are afraid might happen to you and how you would deal with each of them without avoidance.

8. Repeat your fantasy again and again until you begin to feel comfortable with it and increasingly confident that you can implement positive coping strategies.
9. Confront the actual situation that you have practiced confronting in fantasy. Stay in the situation, dealing with your symptoms and thoughts until you experience success in reducing your anxiety in the situation.
10. Make a hierarchical list of real-life situations that you have previously avoided. Imagine yourself in these situations experiencing the same symptoms and thoughts that have previously scared you. Rehearse your active coping strategies by actually using them to reduce your anxiety symptoms and catastrophic thoughts.
11. Again, confront the actual situation that you have been confronting in fantasy.
12. Stop avoiding and start living.

A Consumer's Guide to Treatment

*I*n this chapter, I present information to make you an informed consumer of treatments for panic attacks. Armed with this information, you will be better able to shop for those psychotherapists or physicians who are equipped to help you deal with your problems—if you decide you need professional help. Because panic disorders have only recently been defined adequately enough to develop treatments that specifically target them, there are, in fact, few well-researched, effective interventions. There are even fewer therapists and physicians who have been adequately trained in these approaches. To find those who are, you need to be able to ask informed questions. We will examine what those questions are. We will then examine some of the most popular treatment approaches for dealing with panic attacks, evaluating them according to the published research data.

When to Seek Help

Though the information and techniques provided in this book may go a long way toward helping you deal with your problem of panic, finding professional help is another avenue that you should carefully consider. In fact, obtaining such help and applying the techniques presented here are complementary, not contradictory, strategies; thus, you can seek professional assistance at the same time that you put the techniques presented here into practice. Of course, you may decide you don't need such assistance at this time. Regardless, some guidelines for making such a decision may be helpful:

1. How long have you had your problem? If your panic attacks are relatively recent in origin, having developed in the last six months, you might elect to put off seeking outside help and try implementing the strategies presented here first. Such a decision will likely depend on the next item.

2. How severe are your attacks? Strange as it may seem, a number of people with panic attacks find that they can live with them and never seek treatment. Many have found that their attacks come or go depending on their level of stress and have adjusted their expectations to include intermittent bouts with panic attacks. Usually, such individuals do not experience severe attacks. If your attacks are severe in that you experience a number of symptoms or your attacks last a long time, professional intervention is probably a good idea, even if your attacks have begun only recently.

3. Are your panic attacks scaring you? If they are, professional intervention makes sense. Some people find that they can readily talk themselves out of their catastrophic thoughts or that they really don't believe them in the first place; others find their thoughts really frightening. You are more likely to be in need of outside assistance if your thoughts and fears about your attacks seem out of control. The sooner you get outside help in this case, the better.

4. Do you avoid situations that you associate with panic attacks? If you have begun avoiding situations and if attempts to stop this on your own have failed, you are a good candidate for professional help.

How to Evaluate a Treatment

There are basically four questions to ask when evaluating treatments for panic attacks:

1. What is being treated?
2. How well does the treatment work?
3. What side effects does it have?
4. What is likely to happen when you stop the treatment—in other words, what is its relapse rate?

The effectiveness, side effects, and relapse rates reported in this chapter are composite estimates based on my own review of all available research on this subject.

What Is Being Treated?

By now, you know that your problems with panic derive from several factors. Different treatments target different aspects of panic. Let's briefly review the various aspects. Treatment of panic disorder may focus on:

1. conflicts, stress, or general life problems that may predispose you to panic;
2. the symptoms of panic;

3. catastrophic thoughts that accompany panic;
4. anticipation of panic attacks; and
5. avoidance behavior.

Since specific treatments are more effective with some of these than others, I will point out, if and when such information exists, which treatments target which aspects of panic and how effectively.

How Well Does the Treatment Work?

In other words, "What is the likelihood that your panic attacks and their various aspects will be eliminated or significantly helped by the treatment?" Notice that I include "significantly helped" as one of the possible outcomes of treatment. Seldom do researchers who assess the effectiveness of psychological interventions measure total cure. This satisfaction with less than a total cure is primarily a function of the time limits set for evaluating treatment. Rather than treating panic sufferers until their panic attacks have totally subsided, researchers specify a duration for the treatment, after which they evaluate its effectiveness. This results in a lower estimate of effectiveness than would actually exist in normal clinical practice. You can accordingly expect somewhat better results from actual treatment than I'll be reporting here.

Another factor to be aware of when you go for treatment is that your and your therapist's evaluation of whether the treatment is working after a specific period of time will vary depending on the type of treatment and the problem you are targeting. One guideline you need to keep in mind, therefore, is the time frame within which you can expect improvement. If the problem you are targeting is panic attacks, treatment may be relatively brief. It is likely to last somewhat longer if you are also targeting avoidance behavior. If you are targeting the conflicts or psychological problems that preceded your panic attacks, expect treatment to last still longer.

What Side Effects Does the Treatment Have?

This question applies to both psychotherapy and medications. Most medications produce some side effects, and some produce side effects in most people. Side effects from drugs can be important in two ways:

1. They can include symptoms that are so uncomfortable that you stop treatment or request another treatment.
2. They can produce temporary symptoms that disappear with continued use, or they produce symptoms that develop only with continued use of the drug.

Psychotherapy can produce side effects as a result of the type of treatment being used or the person administering the treatment. Challenging treatments that require you to confront situations you have previously avoided will cause the "side effect" of anxiety. This is natural and to be expected, however, and occurs because the treatment is targeting difficult symptoms. You can therefore expect greater discomfort in the early and middle stages of such treatment, especially if you already avoid specific situations. If the personality of the therapist rather than the type of therapy causes side effects such as higher anxiety or a lower sense of self-worth, you should probably select another therapist. One way to determine if this is happening is to ask yourself if you feel supported by the therapist as he or she pushes you to confront difficult situations. If so, your anxiety is a healthy sign. On the other hand, if you feel demeaned in your efforts to get better, your negative feelings probably reflect your therapist's mishandling of your therapy.

What Is the Relapse Rate of the Treatment?

You should view your problems with panic, and, therefore, your need for treatment, as finite—that is, as coming to an end. If a treatment is effective only while it is ongoing, you should view it with suspicion. Your symptoms of panic are only being suppressed by the treatment and not improving because you are actually changing. Enough is known of the treatment of panic to expect a substantial reduction in the frequency and severity of panic attacks in the majority of cases. Anything less is ineffective treatment. If you avoid a number of situations or if your avoidance has persisted for a year or longer, you should expect treatment to take longer. In such a case, total elimination of your avoidance will help ensure that your problem does not return.

Medication

Five major drug groups are used to treat panic attacks: two groups of antidepressants, two groups of tranquilizers, and the beta-blockers. We will consider each of them separately.

No drug acts on the factors—that is, the underlying conflicts and stress—that predisposes you to panic attacks; medication will not resolve these problems. You may, however, experience some relief from underlying conflict or stress as your general ability to cope improves, your overall anxiety and depression decreases, and you become less preoccupied with having attacks.

If you avoid situations because you fear having panic attacks, you must confront these situations while you are undergoing treatment. The physician treating you should be encouraging you to do so as your attacks subside. If you do not confront these situations, your avoidance will continue, because drugs that reduce panic do not automatically eliminate avoidance behavior. A freqently used approach is to combine medications for panic attacks with some form of psychotherapy designed to help you resolve your conflicts and eliminate your avoidance behavior.

Tricyclic Antidepressants

Antidepressant medications were originally developed to relieve depression but were discovered to relieve panic attacks as well. Some commonly used tricyclic antidepressants, by generic name, include imipramine and amitriptyline (trade names Tofranil and Elavil, respectively). These drugs have the longest history of use in the treatment of panic; therefore, relatively more information is available on them. Dosages typically begin at 25 to 50 milligrams (mg) per day and can be increased to as much as 250 to 300 mg per day. Different people experience relief from their symptoms at different doses. You need to work with your physician to determine the dosage level that relieves your panic symptoms most effectively with the fewest side effects.

Treatment Targets. The tricyclics primarily affect the physical symptoms associated with panic. As these physical symptoms subside, however, the anticipatory anxiety and catastrophic thoughts associated with the symptoms also subside. Anticipatory anxiety takes somewhat longer to ease, subsiding as you gain confidence that you will not have a panic attack. As your anticipatory anxiety eases, if you are encouraged to enter situations you have previously avoided, your avoidance behavior will also decrease.

Expected Effectiveness. If you are able to tolerate tricyclic antidepressants, you have approximately a 63% chance of experiencing significant relief from your symptoms, defined as at least a 50% reduction in the frequency of your panic attacks. Your chances for improvement are slightly better if you do not use avoidance to cope with your panic. Therapeutic effects of tricyclics usually occur slowly, however. Increasing your dosage gradually from 25 mg per day to effective levels of, sometimes, 200 mg or more per day may take several weeks.

Side Effects. These drugs can produce many side effects. Paradoxically, when you first begin to take tricyclics, you are likely to experience symptoms that resemble those of a panic attack, including blurred vision, rapid heart rate, and jitteriness. As your dosage is gradually increased, however, these side effects subside. Because of the severity of these side effects and because people are often insufficiently prepared for them, people often stop taking these drugs before experiencing any benefit. In fact, about a quarter of those who begin taking tricyclic antidepressants stop taking them before gaining control over their panic attacks. Knowing this, you can ask your physician what side effects to expect. Monitoring these effects in yourself and keeping your physician informed of any changes will help you get through the most difficult period of this type of treatment to obtain its maximum benefit.

Relapse. More than 30% of those who stop taking these drugs experience a relapse to the point where they require additional treatment. Moreover, this 30% figure is probably an underestimate, since most of the people evaluated have also been treated with some form of psychotherapy, and psychotherapy itself decreases the chance of a relapse. Accordingly, to decrease your chances of relapse if antidepressants are recommended for your treatment, be sure to also obtain some form of psychotherapy.

Monoamine Oxidase (MAO) Inhibitors

Monoamine oxidase (MAO) Inhibitors were also developed primarily for the treatment of depression. The best-known MAO inhibitor in the treatment of panic is phenelzine (trade name Nardil). Dosage levels of phenelzine for treating panic disorders vary between 45 and 90 mg per day. This group of drugs is prescribed less often, and thus has been evaluated less often, than the tricyclics, primarily because of the dietary restrictions that accompany their use and the dangerous side effects (very high blood pressure) if these dietary restrictions are not adhered to. In spite of these restrictions, however, this group of drugs has a number of advocates, especially because people who are not successfully treated with tricyclics often respond to phenelzine.

Treatment Targets. As with the tricyclics, the primary targets of phenelzine are the physiological responses experienced during panic attacks. If the drug is effective, anticipatory anxiety and catastrophic thoughts will also subside, as a secondary effect. Avoidance behavior is likely to be affected only if you are encouraged to confront the situations you fear.

Expected Effectiveness. Phenelzine is documented as being somewhat less effective than the tricyclics in reducing the symptoms of panic, with a success rate averaging around 58%. As with the tricyclics, you are less likely to respond to the medication if you show patterns of avoidance. Very few studies have examined the effectiveness of these drugs alone, used without some form of psychotherapy or supportive therapy.

Side Effects. Though the side effects are frequent with this drug, there is no published data on the drop-out rate from side effects in studies not involving psychological intervention. Even when supportive therapy is also a part of the treatment package, however, the drop-out rate for those who take phenelzine is approximately 40%, one of the highest among all drug groups. Reasons for this include the necessity for food restrictions (no cheese, red wine, beer, chocolate, or other foods containing tyramine) and the drug's actual side effects (including dry mouth, elevated blood pressure, difficulty sleeping, and difficulty with orgasmic functioning).

Relapse. The relapse rate among individuals who have taken phenelzine is 55%, again one of the highest rates among all drug groups. The reasons for this high rate are unclear, but because it is so high, once you begin taking this drug, you may end up continuing to do so.

Minor Tranquilizers

The minor tranquilizers have been around for a long time and have been studied extensively in relation to the treatment of anxiety in general. The most prominent drugs in this group are diazepam and chlordiazepoxide (Valium and Librium, respectively). Though they have received some attention in the treatment of panic, they now have little following as specific agents in treating this problem.

Treatment Targets. One of the most prominent features of panic attacks is trait, or "background," anxiety. Trait anxiety is a general form of anxiety that includes chronic worry, tension, and jitteriness. This type of anxiety is the principal target of the minor tranquilizers. As we shall see, they are less successful in affecting the symptoms and thoughts that characterize panic attacks. Further, they do not alter anticipatory anxiety or avoidance, primarily because their effect on panic attacks themselves is limited, though they do reduce the level of trait anxiety in some people with panic disorder.

Expected Effectiveness. Minor tranquilizers have been found to be effective for approximately 45% of those who take them. Since this figure is not insignificant, these drugs probably affect panic secondarily, by acting on background anxiety. For the most part, however, researchers studying drug effectiveness have abandoned study of this drug group in relation to treating panic, because the effectiveness rate, compared to other medications, is low.

Side Effects. One of the most prominent side effects of these drugs is that they are physically and psychologically addictive. Of individuals treated with minor tranquilizers for panic attacks, slightly more than 20% drop out of treatment, primarily because of the drugs' lack of effectiveness.

Relapse. No reliable information on the relapse rate after treatment with these drugs ends is available.

High-Potency Benzodiazepines

This drug group is a type of minor tranquilizer, the chief representative of which is alprazolam (Xanax). It has only recently begun to be evaluated as a treatment for panic; because of its immediate apparent success, however, a number of studies have been conducted to assess its effectiveness.

Treatment Targets. Alprazolam specifically affects both the physical symptoms of panic attacks and anticipatory anxiety. It secondarily affects all other aspects of panic. It is given in multiples of 0.25 mg doses, with some individuals responding at doses of 1 mg or less and others requiring as much as 6 to 10 mg a day. Because therapeutic effects are achieved with such low doses, it is considered a high-potency drug.

Alprazolam has the benefit of being fast-acting. People, especially those who respond to low doses, frequently experience a reduction in their symptoms in the first few days after beginning to take the drug. If higher doses are required to bring the panic symptoms under control, relief may take a bit longer, since the usual procedure is to increase the dosage gradually. The same procedure is followed in reverse when coming off the drug.

Expected Effectiveness. Alprazolam has the highest success rate of all antipanic medications, being effective in 68% of the individuals who take it. Its success rate is considerably higher for those without a pattern of avoidance than for those with such a pattern. The most reliable data on the effectiveness of this medication are based on individuals who show some avoidance behavior.

Side Effects. Alprazolam is a fast-acting drug whose effects last a short time. Consequently, you must take it frequently. Because of this, users are more likely to become psychologically addicted, learning to look forward to their next pill. In fact, alprazolam's physical and psychological addictiveness is a major problem with this medication. Going off of this drug should be done gradually and under the strict supervision of your physician.

Aside from its addictiveness, few side effects are associated with this medication: only drowsiness, unsteadiness of gait, and headaches. The drop-out rate is approximately 20%—slightly higher among panic sufferers with avoidance behavior. This indicates that the drug's side effects seldom become problematic enough to discourage users from continuing the drug.

Relapse. Relapse rates for alprazolam are just beginning to be published, and the rates appear to be very high. In one study, more than 80% of the patients had a return of panic attacks during withdrawal from the drug. The average relapse rate across all studies, however, is closer to 40%. Because the panic symptoms return once the level of alprazolam is reduced, many people begun on this medication are reluctant to cut their intake or stop taking the drug.

Beta-Blockers

This group of drugs has received attention in the treatment of panic because of its effect in blocking the excitation of beta-receptors, a type of neuroreceptor found in smooth muscle tissue, such as the heart. Since smooth muscle tissue figures prominently in the symptoms of panic attack sufferers (rapid heart rate, for example), blocking excitation of these organs was considered a possible means of stopping a panic attack. The beta-blocker evaluated in this quest has been propranolol (trade name Inderal), which is prescribed in a daily dosage of 40 to 160 mg.

Treatment Targets. Again, this drug group principally targets those symptoms originating in smooth muscle tissue, such as rapid heart rate and respiratory distress. It also reduces sweating and general tension and is increasing in popularity as a treatment for stage fright among entertainers. Quite incidentally, it may also affect anticipatory anxiety, catastrophic thoughts, and avoidance behavior. No data, however, is currently available to assess its effectiveness with these problems.

Expected Effectiveness. In spite of the rather positive reputation propranolol has in regard to treating panic symptoms, the actual figures are dismal. Only 30% of panic sufferers experience significant improvement from this drug. Further, the rate of success with this treatment is no better among individuals without avoidance behavior than among those with. With or without avoidance, success rates are low.

Beta-blockers are frequently used to treat a physical disorder called mitral valve prolapse syndrome—a usually benign heart defect that causes palpitations. This problem is often associated with panic symptoms, which develop after the disorder has, probably because the principal signs of mitral incompetence are an irregular heartbeat and palpitations. Those who have mitral incompetence may develop panic attacks secondarily, fearing that their problem may lead to more severe difficulties. This represents a small portion of panic sufferers, however, and may not add significantly to propranolol's overall success rate.

Side Effects. The drop-out rate from propranolol is fairly low, averaging approximately 20%. This rate reflects the relatively few side effects of this medication. Propanolol is not recommended, however, if you have lung disease, diabetes, or severe depression. Since the latter frequently accompanies panic attacks, use of propranolol is often precluded.

Relapse. The effect of ending treatment has not been examined for this drug group.

Psychotherapy

There are three general types of approaches to psychotherapeutic treatment of panic disorder:

1. "uncovering" psychotherapies, aimed at identifying and dealing with the conflicts and stresses that may contribute to the development of panic attacks;
2. exposure techniques, aimed at reducing or eliminating the avoidance behavior associated with panic attacks; and
3. psychotherapy aimed at teaching techniques for coping directly with the symptoms of panic.

Most psychotherapists who are acquainted with the research on treating panic disorders and agoraphobia incorporate each of these three approaches in treatment. Appendix A provides a partial list of anxiety treatment clinics throughout the United States that utilize an approach similar to that advocated in this book.

"Uncovering" Psychotherapies

This group is mentioned here simply because it is by far the most common approach you will encounter in seeking help with your panic attacks. Absolutely no data exist, however, on whether these approaches are effective or ineffective in dealing with panic.

Treatment Targets. The goal of this type of approach is to eliminate or reduce the "cause" of the panic attacks and hence eliminate or reduce the attacks indirectly. Treatment is usually long-term, as many of the conflicts and stresses that lead to panic attacks are chronic and difficult to resolve.

One limitation of this type of approach is that, since its practitioners almost always assume an underlying cause, they have difficulty explaining, and, therefore, addressing, panic brought on by medications or caffeine in susceptible persons.

Uncovering psychotherapies may also include reassurance in coping with the panic symptoms and thoughts and encouragement and support in dealing with avoidance behavior. They also might offer specific recommendations on ways of coping with the symptoms of panic. These methods may also be used to address anticipatory anxiety.

Expected Effectiveness. Unknown.

Side Effects. Unknown, but likely to be few unless the approach taken by the therapist is confrontational and abrasive. A reasonable guideline is to get a recommendation for a therapist from a professional whose judgment you trust. Still, if the therapist seems uninformed or possesses a personality that clashes with yours, change therapists!

Relapse. Unknown, since success rates are unknown.

Exposure Techniques

These techniques developed out of the treatment of agoraphobia, the primary feature of which is avoidance. Accordingly, these techniques involve exposing you to situations you have previously avoided, either using imagery or actually putting you in the situations you avoid. Once there, you stay until your symptoms of anxiety subside. Such exposure is repeated until you stop avoiding the situation and feel less anticipatory anxiety in regard to entering the situation. If using imagery, you imagine yourself in the situation until you respond to the imagined

scene with less anxiety. This treatment includes homework assign-
ments that encourage you to enter situations that you have previously
avoided.

Treatment Targets. The primary target is obviously avoidance. A
secondary target is the anticipatory anxiety associated with entering
the situation. Some of these therapies also combine exposure with
cognitive restructuring techniques, which are aimed at changing the
catastrophic cognitions associated with being in the anxiety-provoking
situations. In many cases, panic attacks themselves decrease in the
process of confronting these situations. A variety of approaches that
incorporate exposure as the principal ingredient of treatment has been
shown to be equally effective in reducing panic attacks. These treatments generally ignore conflicts or stressful situations that may
underlie the panic attacks. An exception to this is one school of
thought that identifies conflict-laden marriages as a major contributing factor in agoraphobia. Marital therapy is, accordingly, an integral
part of this treatment approach.

Expected Effectiveness. The overall improvement rate for this type
of treatment with regard to panic attacks is approximately 60%.
Because exposure techniques all target avoidance behavior, their
primary target group has been agoraphobics. This type of approach
is therefore inappropriate if you do not avoid specific situations.

Side Effects. Studies of this type of treatment do not directly measure
side effects. It is well known, however, that both the prospect of confronting and actual confrontation of previously avoided situations temporarily increase anxiety. Approximately 25% of those who try this
type of approach drop out of treatment. Since avoiders generally have
higher drop-out rates than nonavoiders, this rate is relatively low.

Relapse. Approximately 25% of people treated with these methods
experience a return of panic attacks, though this estimate is based
on a small sample and is therefore unreliable. The relapse rate
reportedly declines if clients also receive marital counseling at the
same time. One possible reason for this relapse rate, which, while
good, is not outstanding, is that this approach does not treat panic
attacks directly; rather, significant reductions in the frequency of
panic attacks are a by-product of this treatment. Since I am defining
relapse as the return of panic attacks, the relapse rate is likely at-
tributable to the fact that this approach provides no direct strategies
for dealing with panic.

Coping Approaches

A number of psychological interventions have been developed to teach people to cope with the symptoms and cognitions associated with panic attacks. Typically, practitioners of these approaches emphasize a single coping technique. Some of the more popular strategies include breathing retraining, deep muscle relaxation and other relaxation strategies, and restructuring of catastrophic cognitions. These approaches have begun to be used and tested only in the last few years. Nevertheless, they already represent one of the most promising types of approaches for dealing with panic disorders.

Treatment Targets. These approaches primarily target the symptoms and cognitions that occur during panic attacks. Secondary targets include anticipatory anxiety regarding both attacks and situations as well as avoidance itself. Since the primary target of treatment in this type of approach is the panic attacks themselves, it does not matter whether these attacks can be tied to specific situations or whether they occur spontaneously. This type of approach will work with either.

For the most part, these approaches do not deal with the conflicts and stressors that precede panic attacks. One notable exception is the approach advocated in this book. Though it is true that conflicts and precipitating stressors cannot always be identified, in most cases, they can. When they can be identified, the process of identification and some method of dealing with them can go a long way toward preventing relapse.

Expected Effectiveness. Coping approaches have the highest aggregate rate of improvement of all the interventions presented here—more than 80% of all people treated experience significant improvement, if not the total elimination of all their panic attacks. The improvement rate is higher—approximately 87%—among individuals who do not or only minimally avoid, in contrast to an improvement rate of 66% among individuals with more severe patterns of avoidance. This approach to treatment also significantly reduces avoidance behavior and anticipatory anxiety, though most improvements in these areas occur after the person's panic attacks diminish. Though attacks become less frequent and less severe within one or two weeks, the full benefits of treatment are not gained until the end of therapy. The length of therapy varies with the individual client but averages approximately 10 to 12 weeks, with sessions held once a week.

Side Effects. This type of treatment has minimal side effects, and brings relief extremely quickly. If you have a pattern of avoidance, you will experience a temporary increase in anxiety when confronting situations you avoid. Drop-out rates for these approaches are low, averaging approximately 13%.

Relapse. Relapse following the end of treatment is less than 10%. A number of therapists evaluating these approaches have reported that in follow-up evaluations, most people report that they have had no panic attacks since treatment ended. My own experience in evaluating relapse one and a half years after the end of treatment is that a large percentage of treated individuals continue to experience nearly total relief from the problems that led them to therapy. There are times, however, when panic symptoms recur under stress. Individuals with confidence in their coping skills report that at these times they are able to deal with their symptoms and avoid the catastrophic thinking that previously characterized their attacks.

Integrating Treatment Strategies

There is no reason in our knowledge of panic not to combine treatments to cope with your panic attacks. In fact, if you are already in treatment, your reading this book is an attempt to integrate more than one treatment strategy. The problem, therefore, is not whether to integrate different strategies; rather, the problem is how to integrate strategies.

My assumption throughout this book has been that you want to end up confident in your ability to deal with your panic problem without needing medication. The fact is that many people can be and have been helped without taking any medication whatsoever. A number of you reading this book, however, may already be taking some type of prescription drug. Your task is to gain control over your symptoms, thoughts, and behaviors while simultaneously reducing your medication. This is best accomplished under the direction of your physician, who can help you anticipate problems during your withdrawal from medication. You will probably also benefit from professional psychological assistance during this period. Such assistance can help buttress your resolve to cope with panic on your own while guiding you through the task of developing appropriate strategies.

When beginning treatment, you may elect to use both medication and psychological interventions simultaneously. This is especially the case when your attacks are so overwhelming in their frequency, severity, and duration that coping with them, even with professional assistance, appears impossible. At these times, medication can reduce your attacks to manageable proportions so that you can then work to develop the confidence in your own coping skills that will lead you to eventually master your problems.

Summary

Even though panic disorders have only recently begun to be studied, a great deal is known about them and their treatment. Here are some guidelines for obtaining treatment:

1. Panic disorders and their consequence, agoraphobia, are treatable.
2. The effectiveness of any treatment should be evaluated in relation to how successfully it reduces your symptoms and how likely you are to continue to experience relief after treatment ends. You should also consider the cost of treatment, reckoned in terms of the side effects you suffer, in deciding on a treatment.
3. If you elect to be treated with medication, work closely with your physician. Ask questions and report any change in the symptoms you experience so that you may determine if it is a result of the medication.
4. If you are taking medication, or if medication is recommended, explore the possibility of also receiving psychotherapy, especially if you have a pattern of avoiding situations. Feel free to discuss with your therapist or physician how you can go about reducing and eventually eliminating your medication.
5. Select a psychotherapist who has been recommended as having expertise in treating the type of problem you are having.
6. In selecting a psychotherapist, feel free to ask for an explanation of your problem and a treatment plan for reducing it. Discuss the data presented here to help you decide if the therapist's approach is to your liking.
7. Use what you know; be an informed consumer of treatments for your problem.

Additional Readings

American Psychiatric Association. (1987). *Diagnostic and statistical manual of mental disorders* (rev. 3rd ed.). Washington, DC: Author.

Barlow, D. H., & Cerny, J. A. (1988). *Psychological treatments of panic.* New York: Guilford Press.

Beck, A. T. (1988). Cognitive approaches to panic disorder: Theory and therapy. In S. Rachman & J. D. Mason (Eds.), *Panic: Psychological perspectives* (pp. 91–109). Hillsdale, NJ: Erlbaum.

Beck, A. T., & Emery, G. D. (1985). *Anxiety disorders and phobias: A cognitive perspective.* New York: Basic Books.

Bensen, H. (1975). *The relaxation response.* New York: Avon Books.

Chambless, D. L., Goldstein, A. J., Gallagher, R., & Bright, P. (1986). Integrating behavior therapy and psychotherapy in the treatment of agoraphobia. *Psychotherapy: Theory, Research, and Practice, 23*(1), 150–159.

Clark, D. M., Salkovskis, P. M., & Chalkley, A. J. (1985). Respiratory control as a treatment for panic attacks. *Journal of Behavior Therapy and Experimental Psychiatry, 16,* 23–30.

Clum, G. A. (in press). Psychological interventions vs. drugs in the treatment of panic. *Behavior Therapy.*

Clum, G. A., & Pickett, C. (1984). Panic disorders and generalized anxiety disorders. In H. E. Adams and P. B. Sutker (Eds.), *Comprehensive handbook of psychopathology* (pp. 201–223). New York: Plenum.

Foa, E. B., & Kozak, M. J. (1986). Emotional processing of fear: Exposure to corrective information. *Psychological Bulletin, 99,* 20–35.

Lang, P. J. (1979). A bio-informational theory of emotional imagery. *Psychophysiology, 16,* 495–512.

Mavissakalian, M., & Michelson, L. (1986). Agoraphobia: Relative and combined effectiveness of therapist-assisted in vivo exposure and imipramine. *Journal of Clinical Psychiatry, 47*(3), 117–122.

Michelson, L., Mavissakalian, M., & Marchione, K. (1985). Cognitive and behavioral treatments of agoraphobia: Clinical, behavioral, and psychophysiological outcomes. *Journal of Consulting and Clinical Psychology, 53*(6), 913–925.

Norton, G. R., Harrison, B., Hauch, J., & Rhodes, L. (1985). Characteristics of people with infrequent panic attacks. *Journal of Abnormal Psychology, 94,* 216–221.

Ottaviani, R., & Beck, A. T. (1987). Cognitive aspects of panic disorder. *Journal of Anxiety Disorders, 1,* 15–28.

Rapee, R. (1985). A case of panic disorder treated with breathing retraining. *Journal of Behavior Therapy and Experimental Psychiatry, 16*(1), 63–65.

Sheehan, D. V. (1984). *The anxiety disease.* New York: Schribner's.

Telch, M. J., Agras, W. S., Taylor, C. B., Roth, W. T., & Gallen, C. C. (1985). Combined pharmacological and behavioral treatment for agoraphobia. *Behavior Research and Therapy, 23,* 325–336.

Weekes, C. (1984). *More Help for Your Nerves.* New York: Bantam Books.

Appendix

Listed below, by state, are the names, addresses, and telephone numbers of treatment centers that utilize approaches similar to those advocated in this book.

Arizona
Anxiety, Panic & Phobia Spec.
3337 N. Miller Rd., #105
Scottsdale, AZ 85251
(602) 994-9773
John A. Moran, Ph.D.

Arizona Anxiety Disorder Clinic
1916 W. Anklum Rd.
Tucson, AZ 85745
(602) 792-0165
George Mayo, Ph.D.

California
PhobiaCare Treatment Center
1420 Cooley Dr., Ste. 110
Colton, CA 92324
(714) 877-8716

A CHAANGE Affiliate
5588 North Palm Ave.
Fresno, CA 93704
(209) 435-9500
Mark H. Seyer, Ph.D., MFCC

Phobia & Anxiety Disorders Center
410 Arden Ave., Ste. 201
Glendale, CA 91203
(818) 502-0513

Phobia Treatment Program
22300 Foothill Blvd., Ste. M14
Hayward, CA 94541
(415) 886-0512
Joan Wickstrand &
    Charles Wickstrand

PhobiaCare Treatment Center
18682 Beach Blvd., Ste. 210
Huntington Beach, CA 92648
(714) 832-8838

Phobia & Anxiety Treatment Center
836 Prospect, Ste. 201
La Jolla, CA 92037
(619) 456-5065
Marjorie F. Coburn, Ph.D.

Anxiety Disorders Clinic
Graduate Hall
LAC-USC Medical Center
1937 Hospital Pl.
Los Angeles, CA 90033
(213) 226-5329

Behavioral Science Associates
1100 Glendon Ave., Ste. 1427
Los Angeles, CA 90024
(213) 824-5314

TERRAP Phobia Program
941 Westwood Blvd., Ste. 237
Los Angeles, CA 90024
(213) 836-6445

TERRAP Phobia Clinic
1120 Crane St., Ste. 15
Menlo Park, CA 94025
(415) 321-0300

Institute for Phobic
    Awareness
1472 San Jacinto Way
P. O. Box 1180
Palm Springs, CA 92262
(619) 322-COPE
Dr. Marilyn J. Gellis, Dir.

Life Skills
3550 Watt Ave., Ste. 140
Sacramento, CA 95821
(916) 482-1174
Renau Z. Peurifoy, M.A., MFCC

Sacramento Phobia Clinic
225 30th St., Ste. 208
Sacramento, CA 95821
(916) 344-4314

Behavioral Medicine Systems
2710 Health Center Dr., Ste. C
San Diego, CA 92123
(619) 571-1188

Mesa Vista Hospital
Anxiety Disorders Program
7850 Vista Hill Ave.
San Diego, CA 92123
(619) 694-8300

Hypnosis & Behavioral Medicine
    Clinic
2351 Clay, Ste. 311
San Francisco, CA 94115
(415) 923-3594
Jill Bond Caire, Ph.D.

San Francisco Panic-Phobia
    Treatment Center
1801 Bush St., #114
San Francisco, CA 94109
(415) 931-6119

Phobia Counseling Center
1745 Saratoga Ave.

San Jose, CA 95129
(408) 255-6911
Bernard M. Sjoberg, Ph.D., Dir.

San Fernando Valley Treat-
    ment Center for Anxiety
    Disorders
13701 Riverside Dr., #508
Sherman Oaks, CA 91423
(818) 789-0564

PhobiaCare Treatment Center
14101 Yorba St., Ste. 105
Tustin, CA 92680
(714) 832-8838

Colorado
Bruce Brian, Ph.D.
911 North Corona
Colorado Springs, CO 80903
(303) 634-7500

Phobia & Anxiety Treatment
    Center
2850 Serendipity Circle
Colorado Springs, CO 80907
(303) 570-7878

Phobia Treatment Center
777 S. Wadsworth Blvd.
Irongate 4
Lakewood, CO 80226
(303) 988-5706

Connecticut
Yale Anxiety Research Clinic
34 Park St.
New Haven, CT 06508
(203) 789-7334

Pain Management & Behavior
    Therapy Center
567 Vauxhall St. Ext.
Waterford, CT 06359
(203) 443-4343

Delaware
Marsha Orlov, Ed.D., &
    Leland G. Orlov, Ph.D.
1601 Milltown Rd.
Lindell Square #7
Wilmington, DE 19808
(302) 994-4014

District of Columbia
Agoraphobia & Anxiety Program
Department of Psychology
American University
Washington, DC 20016
(202) 885-1711

National Center for the Treatment of Phobias & Anxiety
1755 S St., NW
Washington, DC 20009
(202) 363-7792

Florida
Atlantic Counseling Center
403 N. Wild Olive Ave.
Daytona Beach, FL 32018
(904) 253-2531
William P. Friedenberg, Ph.D., Dir.

Fair Oaks Hospital Anxiety
    Clinic
5440 Linton Blvd.
Delray Beach, FL 33445
(305) 495-3788

Phobia, Anxiety & Psycho-
    therapy Center
3716 University Blvd. S.,
    Ste. 6B
Jacksonville, FL 32216
(904) 739-3688
Alan J. Harris, Ph.D.

Behavioral Medicine Clinic
1114 East Tennessee St.
Tallahassee, FL 32308
(904) 222-2291
Jay Mulkerne, Ph.D.

Georgia
Atlanta Area Phobia Program
25B Lenox Pointe
Atlanta, GA 30324
(404) 266-8881
Charles Melville, Ph.D., Dir.

Atlanta Phobia & Anxiety Clinic
Medical Quarters, Ste. 106
5555 Peachtree-Sunabody Rd.
Atlanta, GA 30342
(404) 256-0802

Augusta Area Anxiety &
    Agoraphobia Clinic
2350 Washington Rd.
Augusta, GA 30904
(404) 733-9616
Henry F. Ball, M.D.

Illinois
Anxiety Disorders Clinic
University of Health Sciences,
Department of Psychology
Chicago Medical School, Bldg. 51
North Chicago, IL 60064
(312) 578-3305
Richard J. McNally, Ph.D

Anxiety Disorders Clinic
Department of Psychiatry &
    Behavioral Medicine
University of Illinois
College of Medicine
7725 North Knoxville
Peoria, IL 61614
(309) 671-8222

Kansas
Anxiety Disorders Clinic
Memorial Hospital
600 Madison
Topeka, KS 66607
(913) 354-5373

Kentucky
Linder Psychological Services
2886 Brownsboro Rd.
Louisville, KY 40206
(502) 897-9950

Louisiana
Tulane University Medical Center
Department of Psychiatry &
Neurology
1415 Tulane Ave.
New Orleans, LA 70112
(504) 588-5405

Maryland
Facing Fears: Phobia Treatment
    Program of Psychological
    Services
111 Annapolis St.
Annapolis, MD 21401
(301) 263-8255

New Ventures Phobia Center
3501 Moylan Dr.
Bowie, MD 20715
(301) 464-2622
Jon E. Williams, Ph.D., Dir.

Cognitive Therapy Center
4701 Willard Ave., Ste. 222
Chevy Chase, MD 20815
(301) 951-3828

Phobia Treatment Center of
  Chevy Chase
2 Wisconsin Circle,
  Ste. 700
Chevy Chase, MD 20815
(301) 654-3565

Sheppard-Pratt Hospital
Anxiety Disorders Program
6501 N. Charles St.
Towson, MD 21204
(301) 938-4900
Sally Winston, Psy.D.

Massachusetts
Agoraphobia Treatment Center
  of New England
264 Beacon St.
Boston, MA 02116
(617) 262-5223

Behavior Associates
45 Newbury St.
Boston, MA 02116
(617) 262-8116

Fear Clinic
670 Washington St.
Braintree, MA 02184
(617) 843-7550

Behavior Associates
7 Federal St.
Danvers, MA 01923
(617) 774-0142

Behavior Consultants
8 Madaket Pl., Ste. B
Mashpee, MA 02649
(508) 477-6020
Jane P. McNally, Ph.D., Dir.

Exposure Therapy & Counseling
  Services
20 Maple St.
Springfield, MA 01105
(413) 733-2034

Steven C. Fischer, Psy.D.
24 Wildwood Ln.
Sudbury, MA 01776
(508) 443-5747

Michigan
Anxiety Disorders Program
University of Michigan
  Medical Center
1500 E. Medical Center Dr.
Ann Arbor, MI 48109-0840
(313) 764-5348

TERRAP of Michigan
103 College SE
Grand Rapids, MI 49503
(616) 774-0066

Missouri
Anxiety Disorder Clinic
14377 Woodlake Dr., #212
Chesterfield, MO 63017
(314) 576-7454
Ira H. Dubinsky, Ph.D., Dir.

Anxiety Disorders Center
St. Louis University Medical
  Center
1221 S. Grand Blvd.
St. Louis, MO 63104
(314) 577-8702

New Jersey
Anxiety Disorders Program
Carrier Foundation
Belle Mead, NJ 08502
(201) 874-4000

Fort Lee Consultation Center
2015 Center Ave.
Fort Lee, NJ 07024
(201) 944-5889

William J. O'Connor, Ed.D., P.A.
1700 Whitehorse-Hamilton
  Square Rd., Ste. B5
Hamilton Square, NJ 28690-2718
(609) 586-1586

New Jersey Institute for Stress
  & Anxiety Reduction
TERRAP
652 Middlesex Ave.
Metuchen, NJ 08840
(201) 906-1919

Behavior Therapy Center
206 Main St., Ste. 22
Millburn, NJ 07041
(201) 376-6062

Anxiety/Phobia Treatment Center
129 Valley Rd.
Montclair, NJ 07042
(201) 744-3178

Behavioral Health Center
34 Crest View Rd.
Mountain Lakes, NJ 07046
(201) 335-5255

Behavior Therapy Service
University of Medicine &
  Dentistry of New Jersey
Community Mental Health Center
215 S. Orange Ave.
Newark, NJ 07103
(201) 456-4869

Affiliates in Psychotherapy
600 New Road, Atlantic County
Northfield, NJ 08225
(609) 641-2500

Wayne Psychological Group
330 Ratzer Rd., Ste. 25
Wayne, NJ 07470
(201) 696-6656
Emile B. Gurstelle, Ph.D.

New York
Albany Psychological
  Associates, P.C.
1215 Western Ave., Ste. 104
Albany, NY 12203
(518) 438-0037

Phobia Treatment Center
21 Campbell Road Ct.
Binghamton, NY 13905
(607) 723-5249
Richard H. Normile, Ph.D.

Institute for Behavior Therapy
83 Ryder Rd.
Briarcliff Manor, NY 10510
(914) 762-2986
William Golden, Ph.D.

Hillside Hospital-Long Island
  Jewish Hospital Center
Box 38
Glen Oaks, NY 11004
(718) 470-8120

Institute for Behavior Therapy
9 Northern Blvd.
Greenvale, NY 11548
(516) 621-3322

Phobic Clinic of Peninsula
  Counseling Center
270 Lawrence Ave.
Lawrence, NY 11559
(516) 239-1945
Marsha Wagman, CSN, Dir.

Phobia Center
265 East Lake Blvd.
Mahopoc, NY 10541
(914) 628-5456

Phobia Center
245 E. 87th St., Ste. 17G
New York, NY 10128
(212) 860-5560
Carol Lindemann, Ph.D.

Phobia Clinic
Lakeland Dr.
South Fallsburg, NY 12779
(914) 434-6465

Phobia Clinic
White Plains Hospital
  Medical Center
Davis Ave. at Post Rd.
White Plains, NY 10601
(914) 681-1038

North Carolina
Center for Behavioral Medicine
4000 Blue Ridge Rd., Ste. 350
Raleigh, NC 27612
(919) 781-1707

Ohio

Phobia Clinic, University Hospital
Hanna Pavilion
2040 Abington Rd.
Cleveland, OH 44106
(216) 844-7840

Phobia Clinic of Toledo
5800 Monroe St., Bldg. B
Sylvania, OH 43560
(419) 882-7189
c/o Joel M. Kestenbaum, Ph.D.

Midwest Center for Stress
 & Anxiety
3900 Sunforest Ct., #212
Toledo, OH 43623
(419) 898-4357

Oregon

Anxiety Disorders Clinic
4550 SW Kruse Way, Ste. 325
Lake Grove, OR 97035
(503) 635-8710

Center for Anxiety Treatment
2188 Southwest Park Pl.
Portland, OR 97205
(503) 274-4229

Portland Agoraphobia Center
2104 NW Everett
Portland, OR 97210
(503) 222-1426

Portland Phobia Clinic
319 SW Washington
Spalding Bldg., Ste. 1001
Portland, OR 97205
(503) 223-6765
Carole Lansdowne, Ph.D.

Pennsylvania

Frank M. Dattilio, Ph.D., &
 Cary S. Rothstein, Ph.D.
1251 S. Cedar Crest Blvd., #211D
Allentown, PA 18103
(215) 432-5066

Agoraphobia & Anxiety Treatment
 Center of Temple University
112 Bala Ave.
Bala Cynwyd, PA 19004
(215) 667-6490

Lehigh Phobia Program
Department of Psychology
Bldg. 17
Lehigh University
Bethlehem, PA 18015
(215) 758-362
S. Lloyd Williams, Ph.D., Dir.

Chalfont Psychological Associates
1A Highland Dr.
Chalfont, PA 18914
(215) 822-7829
Cary S. Rothstein, Ph.D.

Stress & Anxiety Disorder Clinic
Department of Behavioral
 Medicine
Geisinger Medical Center
Danville, PA 17822
(717) 271-6516

Anxiety & Phobic Disorder Clinic
Lancaster Counseling Center
1024 N. Duke St.
Lancaster, PA 17602
(717) 299-5106

Anxiety Treatment Center
2817 West Ridge Pike
Trooper, PA 19403
(215) 539-0484

Tennessee

Vanderbilt Mood Disorders
 Program
Anxiety Disorders Clinic
Vanderbilt Clinic
22nd Ave. S, 3rd fl., Rm. 3942
Nashville, TN 37232
(615) 322-0387

Texas

Lester Harrell, Ph.D.
1000 E. 32nd St., Ste. 3
Austin, TX 78705
(512) 476-4208

Laboratory for the Study of
 Anxiety Disorders
Department of Psychology,
Mezes 330
University of Texas
Austin, TX 78712
(512) 471-3722

Phobia Center of Dallas/Fort Worth
4307 Newton Ct., Ste. 11
Dallas, TX 75219
(214) 522-6181
(Fort Worth Metro Area toll-free:
  (817) 461-7357)

Phobia Centers of the Southwest
12860 Hillcrest Rd., Ste. 119
Dallas, TX 75230
(214) 386-6681

Phobia Center of Forth Worth
2108 West 6th, Ste. 22
Fort Worth, TX 76201
(817) 335-3327

TERRAP Phobia Treatment Center
  (TERRAP, Texas)
14 Greenway Plaza #4–Q
Houston, TX 77046
(713) 871-1145

Utah

Clinic for Phobias & Anxiety
  Disorders
Department of Psychology
University of Utah
501 Chipeta Way
Salt Lake City, UT 84109
(801) 583-2500
Mark E. Owens, Ph.D.

Virginia

Roundhouse Phobia Treatment
  Center
1444 Duke St.
Alexandria, VA 22314
(703) 836-7131

James W. Eisenhower, LCSW
732 Thimble Shoals Blvd.
Newport News, VA 23606
(804) 873-1861

Anxiety Disorders Program
St. Albans Psychiatric Hospital
P. O. Box 3608
Radford, VA 24143
(703) 639-2481, Ext. 220 or 361

Washington

Norbstrom Medical Tower
1229 Madison, Ste. 890
Seattle, WA 98104
(206) 386-2200
Arthur W. Peskind, Ph.D.

Seattle Phobia Clinic
901 Boren Ave.
Cabrin: Medical Tower
Seattle, WA 98104
(206) 343-9474
Gerald M. Rosen, Ph.D.,
  Clinical Psychologist

Arthur W. Peskind, Ph.D.
1530 S. Union Ave., Ste. 16
Tacoma, WA 98405
(206) 752-7320

West Virginia

TERRAP West Virginia
Phobia Treatment Program
P. O. Box 383
Wheeling, WV 26003
(304) 232-2996
(In-state: 1-800-441-1231)

Wisconsin

Phobia Institute of Milwaukee
759 N. Milwaukee St., Ste. 612
Milwaukee, WI 53202
(414) 276-6988

To the owner of this book:

I hope that you have been significantly influenced by reading *Coping with Panic*. I'd like to know as much about your experiences with the book as you care to offer. Your comments can help us make it a better book for future readers.

1. What I like most about this book is _____

   _____

2. What I like least about this book is _____

   _____

3. Specific topics in the book I thought were most relevent and important

   are _____

   _____

4. Specific suggestions for improving the book: _____

   _____

   _____

Optional:

Your name: _____ Date: _____

May Broo~ ~ with Panic
or in futu

Yes ____

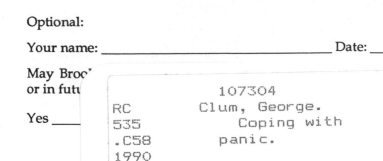

DATE DUE

NO POSTAGE
NECESSARY
IF MAILED
IN THE
UNITED STATES

B
F

POST

ATT:

Bro
511
Pac

FOLD HI

FOLD HERE